Retail Banking

TECHNOLOGY

Retail Banking

TECHNOLOGY

The Smart Way to Serve Customers

SURESH SAMUDRALA

JAICO PUBLISHING HOUSE

Ahmedabad Bangalore Bhopal Bhubaneswar Chennai
Delhi Hyderabad Kolkata Lucknow Mumbai

Published by Jaico Publishing House
A-2 Jash Chambers, 7-A Sir Phirozshah Mehta Road
Fort, Mumbai - 400 001
jaicopub@jaicobooks.com
www.jaicobooks.com

RETAIL BANKING TECHNOLOGY
ISBN 978-81-8495-682-5

First Jaico Impression: 2015

Page design and layout: Bharati Composers, Delhi

Printed by

Foreword

In the late nineties, during the dot com euphoria days, a slogan "We Need Banking – Not Banks" was floating around. It reflected a mood that all non-real goods would get digitized and moved over networks. It was a technological possibility. But it did not happen with the speed with which it could have happened, or at least as fast as many would have liked it to happen.

Banks deal with funds of depositors and as such cannot risk deploying new solutions unless they are fully tested and accepted. Therefore, they have adopted the strategy of "Slow but Steady". The banks designed, developed and delivered technology-based products, services and delivery channels gradually, along with the necessary security systems around them. The security systems give confidence to both internal as well as external users. Trust is the key ingredient of banking.

Technology can increase operational efficiency, reduce transaction costs and more importantly enhance customer experience. While the first two are not easily measurable, customer experience is quite visible. Among various segments of banking, retail banking deals with the customer experience the most. Over the past two decades, Indian banks focused on improving retail banking services with the adoption of appropriate information technology solutions.

ATMs, Internet Banking and Mobile Banking brought banking closer to the customer. Today, banks are providing interfaces to banking through social media networks. Retail banking is progressively moving towards realization of the slogan of the nineties.

There have been so many developments in the area of retail banking; it is difficult to get a full picture of all of them easily. It is in this context the book, *Retail Banking Technology*, would be helpful. Samudrala has brought out the developments in retail banking technology in Indian banks in this book, by presenting the products, services and delivery channels quite comprehensively. I feel that his well-organized and easy-to-read book would be useful to get initiated into the subject.

Dr. A. S. Ramasastri
Director
Institute for Development and Research
in Banking Technology, Hyderabad

Preface

Banking and financial services organizations are the largest consumers of information technology deploying a large IT workforce worldwide. Banks have a complex landscape of technology and applications catering to their diverse information needs. These applications have a lot of inter-dependencies and they exchange information through a complex set of interfaces. There are millions of employees working on various technology jobs for banks across the world. However, technology staff will typically get to work in one particular application or a functional area. It is very important for them to understand at a high level the overall technology landscape and context of their application in that landscape. Knowledge of upstream and downstream system interfaces and their criticality will help them appreciate the overall business relevance and criticality of their particular area/application. This book is targeted towards the technology staff working in banks to provide them an overview of the entire IT landscape and to help them understand the context of their application/area.

Obviously, each bank has variations in its technology and no two banks in the world are the same in terms of technology landscape. Some banks have a more advanced technology than others. Also, there are country specific variations in banking features, products and payment systems. This book attempts to capture the technology landscape in the most common and generic way possible so that readers can relate to it irrespective of their current location or landscape.

Information presented in this book is for education and knowledge purposes only and is not intended to recommend any target architecture or product. This book is aimed as a guide or knowledge source. This book is Part 1 of a three book series and is focused on retail banking. Part 2 and Part 3 will focus on investment banking and corporate banking technologies respectively.

Feedback and suggestions from readers will be highly appreciated to improve the quality of the content of future versions/books.

Please reach out to me at my e-mail id - author@ bankingtechnologyguide.com for any interaction/feedback/suggestions on this project.

Suresh Samudrala

Acknowledgements

I am grateful to all my friends and colleagues who inspired me to attempt something different. I would like to thank my parents and family for supporting me in all my endeavours. I would also like to thank the publishing team for the guidance and support they provided in this project.

I take this opportunity to thank Prof. M. Subramanyam, GITAM School of International Business for providing review support for this project. I also would like thank Dr. A.S. Ramasastri, Director, Institute for Development and Research in Banking Technology (IDRBT) for providing an insightful Foreword for this project.

Contents

CHAPTER 1
Introduction

Banking and financial services organizations are one of the largest consumers of information technology and they deploy a large Information Technology (IT) workforce worldwide. Their businesses are built around specialized knowledge and information processing. In the banking industry, product design, product marketing, product distribution and product servicing take place using IT systems. Technology enables banks to create new products, provide superior customer experience, comply with regulations and manage staff effectively. In today's world, technology offers significant competitive advantages for banks to streamline and automate their operations thus reducing costs while enhancing their capability to scale up for higher volumes. Information technology forms an integral part of a bank's strategy as an enabler for optimization, customer experience and innovation irrespective of its current level of technological sophistication. Emerging technologies challenge the existing models of selling and servicing various products and hence continuous investment in technology becomes mandatory for banks to retain a leading position in industry. It is fair to say that no bank in the world is able to take up any major or minor business initiative without enhancing or at least considering its impact on their technology.

Banks have a complex technology landscape consisting of reliable data centres, significant hardware and software infrastructure as well as a diverse set of applications. A bank's technology forms a significant part of the overall cost base with various cost elements like data centre space, infrastructure costs, software license costs, annual maintenance contract costs, and manpower costs for running the IT systems as well as their enhancements. Banking applications cater to the needs of various stakeholders such as senior management, branch staff, operations staff, marketing, risk management, HR teams as well as customers. Some of the characteristics of banking applications are the ability to process high volumes of transactions, handle large volumes of concurrent users/customers and large volumes of transaction/analytical data. It is critical for banking applications to be readily available, provide reliable service/response times and have near-zero severity defects. Due to the complexity, only a small architecture group has an overview of the technology landscape, which is impossible for most of the IT staff. Considering the business criticality, it is important for the IT staff working in one application or area of the bank to have a complete overview of the overall IT landscape and interfaces, in order to be able to appreciate their area of specialization better. This books aims to provide a bird's eye view of the landscape for easy understanding of the various applications and interfaces and the dependencies between them.

Another key focus area of this book is explanation of the key technology concepts in the context of banking technology. In the last decade or so, several new technologies have come into prominence such as Service Oriented Architecture (SOA), Master Data Management (MDM), Customer Relationship Management (CRM), Business Process Management (BPM), Web Content Management Systems (WCM), Document Management Systems (DMS) etc. These products are provided by various technology vendors and have been widely adopted across several organizations including banks. Each of these technologies have specialist teams handling the technology rollout within the banks, however it is important for other employees to understand how these technologies work and see the benefits these technologies bring in. This book makes an attempt to elaborate on the usage of such technologies across different functional applications within the banking technology landscape. This will give the readers a practical understanding of how these technologies work and the possible areas within a bank where these technologies are used.

Banking services are broadly categorized into the following three areas:

- **Retail banking:** Serving retail customers, offering savings, deposits and loans.
- **Business and corporate banking:** Serving small, medium and large enterprises, offering current accounts, payments, cash management, trade finance, guarantees and Foreign Exchange (FOREX) services.

- **Investment banking:** Capital market related services like advisory, investment research, brokerage, mergers & acquisitions and wealth management

This is the first of a three book series, and it focuses on the landscape of retail banking technology. In this book, concepts of banking technology are explained in practical and simple terms for easy and comprehensive understanding of the IT landscape. It is targeted towards persons currently working in a bank's IT department or those who are planning take up a job in this field. The technology landscape varies significantly from one bank to another. Strategic importance and investments assigned to IT will ultimately determine the maturity of the IT infrastructure, whether it is based on legacy technologies or strategic platforms or a combination of both. The technology landscape of large global banks can be highly complex with multiple instances/versions of various IT components catering to different functions in different geographies. Also, the technology landscape of banks in different countries can vary depending on the retail services, payment infrastructure and market practices. This book aims to cover the generic and current technology principles of retail banking applicable across the various banks and geographies that readers can relate to.

THE IMPORTANCE OF BANKS

Some of the reasons why it is necessary to focus on the banking industry, what is the importance of the banking industry to a country's economy and why it is highly regulated unlike other industries, are given below:

- Directly or indirectly, banks ultimately hold all the money that any individual or corporate owns. Banks enable easy and smooth transfer of money from one party to another. Money continuously flows from one party to another and in the reverse direction of the flow of goods or services. Movement of money is directly proportional to the movement of goods and services and in turn to the industrial activity in that country. By enabling a smooth flow of money, banks form the back bone of a country's growth.

- It is essential for the economy to have financially strong banks. By the very nature of their business, banks are structurally weak corporate houses due to very high leverage. Leverage in simple terms is the ratio of borrowed money vs. equity capital. Banks can be seen as having a very high leverage due to the fact that a large part of customer deposits are used for lending as long as mandatory capital requirements/statutory regulations are met. Due to the high leverage as compared to other industries, banks are often referred to as 'conditionally solvent'. Account holders/ depositors have the right to withdraw funds at any time but no bank will survive if all the depositors of the bank come at the same time to withdraw deposits. Also, non-performing assets (loans disbursed but not getting repaid) will erode the capital, and any systemic event that results in large defaults (e.g., the mortgage crisis in the US) will put the banking system, and in turn all the individuals and corporate houses in that country, under severe pressure. This is one of the main reasons for very high regulation in the banking industry.

- In a positive economic environment banks create a domino effect causing the overall economy to grow significantly. The banks' balance sheet growth and credit growth will directly map to the economic growth. For every deposit received, banks will be able to lend what is left after provisioning for the mandatory cash reserve (minimum cash to be held with the central bank) and statutory liquidity (minimum percentage of deposits to be maintained in liquid form) norms. Typically, banks will be able to lend up to 70 per cent of the deposits received provided they are able to maintain the required capital, and the entire amount of money lent will come back to the banking system directly or indirectly. With appropriate addition of capital, banks will be able to again lend that amount and this cycle will continue with expansion of banks' balance sheets in the process. Banks are at the heart of all economic activity and hence an efficient banking system will make the money move faster resulting in increased credit growth and increased balance sheets, leading to increased economic growth.

- Banks offer various services for business and corporate customers which enable them to service their customers and complete their transactions quickly and smoothly. Services offered by banks to small and medium businesses, such as current accounts with overdraft facilities, trade finance and payment solutions, promote trade and help firms conduct their business efficiently. Banks acquire merchants and provide them with a point of sale devices, allowing their customers to use credit or debit cards for payment. Banks offer working capital loans for businesses to help them with cash flows during product lifecycle. Banks offer services related to FOREX as well as export/import transactions in the form of documentary credits to enable simple and risk free trade with their counterparts across the globe. These services enable growth in trade and financial activities, boosting the economy.

- Sometimes governments use banks as a tool for promoting inclusive and broad-based growth. Governments set minimum limits for lending to priority sectors like agriculture, small and medium businesses, education etc. Government and national central banks review these limits from time to time to ensure credit growth to priority sectors.

- Central banks control the monetary policy and circulation of money in the banking system. Monetary policy has an overwhelming influence on the flow of money and in turn on the operations of the bank. Central banks can take an inflationary monetary stance to propel growth by making it easy for circulation of money in the system. This means a period of low interest rates and high growth. On the other hand when the system is overheated, central banks can take anti-inflationary measures resulting in an environment of high interest rates and low growth. Thus banks are an integral part of the Central Bank's strategy for monetary policy.

Having briefly covered the importance and implications of banks in the overall economy, we now look at some of the key functions within a retail bank.

RETAIL BANKING

Retail banking can be divided into units based on some of the following categories:

- **Customer segmentation:** Retail organization may be further divided based on customer segmentation like basic, privilege, student, salaried, women, high-net worth etc. This approach lays emphasis on customer focus and improves the potential for cross-selling of products based on the broad segment needs.
- **Products:** Retail banking may be further sub-divided based on the product offerings such as deposits, retail credit cards, personal loans and home loans. This approach is more product focused and builds on specific product knowhow.
- **Regional/geography:** Retail banking may be sub-divided based on the geographical regions of the operating branches. This is more relevant for the global banks as well as countries with vast geographical spread and banking needs that vary significantly across regions.

There are a number of divisions in retail banking, each headed by a senior manager.

Head of Retail Banking

The head of retail banking deals with the retail portfolio and its profitable growth.

Head of Banking Operations

Banking operations include managing the operations and seeing to the smooth functioning of the same. Some of the responsibilities of the head of banking operations are:

- Managing back office operations
- Managing customer contact centres
- Property management
- Legal issues

Chief Financial Officer (CFO)

This functionary is responsible for the financials of a bank including:

- Budgeting
- Accounts management

- Accounts payable, receivables
- Financial statements etc.

Head of Technology (CIO)

The CIO is responsible for the technology landscape of the bank and ensuring that it is fit-for-purpose, available, stable and can be enhanced as per business requirements within the budgets and timelines. One of the key responsibilities of the CIO is to have a close alignment with business and ensure that technology programs meet those expectations. The Head of Technology plays a very critical role and reflects the importance attached to IT as a strategic investment. Organizations that have viewed IT as strategic capability and invested accordingly have significantly benefitted from it.

Head of Credit

The Head of Credit is responsible for implementing the credit policies of the bank. This includes credit decisions, credit monitoring and collections operations. Centralized credit decisions include customer scoring based credit approval. Credit monitoring includes customer behavioural scoring based analysis of potential defaulters and taking proactive measures. The collections process includes arriving at an effective strategy to deal with 'out of order' accounts.

Head of Human Resources (HR)

Employees are one of the most important components of a knowledge industry like banking. HR is primarily responsible for hiring the best talent, retaining that talent, managing the performance according to organizational goals, managing employee welfare, and processing the payroll and other benefits for employees.

Head of Marketing

The Head of Marketing is responsible for establishing the brand, connecting with existing and potential customers with opportunities to sell/cross-sell, conduct promotional events to target new customers etc.

RETAIL BANKING PRODUCTS

Some of the most common products offered by retail banks are generally well understood and common to most banks, although the features offered by different products from different banks may vary.

- **Accounts:** Offers basic account services to customers like salary accounts, student accounts etc.
- **Deposits:** Offers deposit products to customers like term deposits, recurring deposits, etc.
- **Payments:** Offers payments services like cheque processing, bill payments, ATMs, debit cards etc.
- **Credit cards:** Offers credit cards to customers as a convenient payment option and unsecured credit.
- **Mortgages:** Offers loans to its customers to purchase homes.
- **Car loans:** Offers loans to its customers to purchase automobiles.
- **Unsecured loans:** Offers its customers other kinds of unsecured loans like personal loans, educational loans etc.

The above mentioned key banking functions and products require significant information and depend heavily on IT systems to address those needs. A bank's IT infrastructure should be able to cater to the needs of these functions in an efficient and cost predictable manner. Retail banks have to deal with a large number of customers, usually in millions, who will transact with the bank on their accounts/ products resulting in several million transactions a day. Technology has to be designed to make sure these transactions happen in a timely manner and in an automated fashion with minimal/no manual intervention. Various channels like ATMs, internet banking and more recently mobile banking have brought significant efficiencies to banking operations, apart from a world of convenience to customers. Banks need to continuously look for the bottlenecks that require manual intervention and find ways to reduce or eliminate such manual efforts. This requires optimization of business processes and the underlying technology.

Retail banking is about relationships with customers. Well serviced customers will provide life time business and many opportunities to cross sell products. Retail banking is about steady and consistent offerings to customers. IT plays a major role in achieving these objectives by providing the ability to design, market, sell and service the banking products as per business strategy. This book covers the key functionalities of the IT systems that help banks achieve those objectives.

CHAPTER 2
Technology Landscape

Assuming that one is starting a new retail bank, what infrastructure and IT systems are needed? Who will access these systems and from where? What does the landscape look like? In this chapter we give answers to some of these questions.

INFRASTRUCTURE LANDSCAPE

The first thing that comes to mind, when we talk about a bank's infrastructure, is the branches of the bank. A branch is the face of the bank for many customers. Braches are predominantly used for all important activities like opening an account, advice and transactions. Another popular access point for banks are ATMs and one can usually find more ATMs than branches at any particular location. ATMs provide basic transaction services and are available nearly 24x7, much beyond branch operating hours. Banks also have a head office and various regional offices for the bank's management and support functions staff. This is where the key decisions are made and various operations are monitored and tracked. Central operation centres of a bank are usually set up to centralize certain business processes like customer contact centres, processing cheques, printing statements, dispatch etc. These centres are usually large and service the staff facing the customers across braches as well as customers in the designated function. Finally, banks have data centres to host all the hardware infrastructure like processors, storage, network equipment and business applications.

Figure 2.1 presents an overview of a bank's infrastructure landscape.

As already discussed, properties owned/leased by a bank can be categorized as:

- Branches
- ATMs

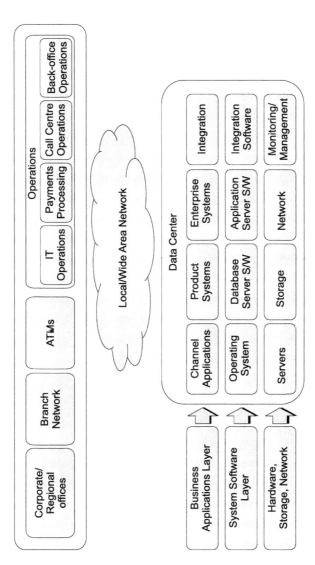

Fig. 2.1 *Bank Infrastructure*

- Corporate office/Regional offices
- Central operations centre
- Data centre

We will look at these infrastructure elements in more detail to understand the considerations involved in their design.

Branches

Initially branches were the only mode of interaction between customers and banks. Even with the advent of various electronic channels to access banking services, a branch still plays a major role in acquiring customers and servicing them, as well as building the brand. Branch locations are carefully chosen according to the customer profile of the bank and are predominantly located in prime areas. The size of a branch depends on the expected customer footfall and the range of services provided in the branch. Branches in prime localities of major towns and cities will be much larger and have more staff compared to rural branches or extension branches that could typically run with one or two staff members.

A branch is designed after carefully considering the branch strategy, customer experience, optimized branch staff, product mix offered and use of technology. These considerations are elaborated below:

- **Branch strategy:** Large banks with a significant customer base may prefer to drive customers towards self-service channels for basic services to optimize the cost of servicing the customers. They may take some measures to discourage branch banking for basic transactions, like charging a small fee for cash transactions in the branch. However, small and upcoming banks may want to use the branch as a medium to meet their customers, understand their needs and offer them a better experience so as to improve their share apart from exploring cross-sell opportunities.

- **Customer experience:** Customers visiting the branch would like to have their transactions completed quickly and smoothly. Availability of in-branch ATMs, kiosks, telephone banking dock, display of interest rates and other related information will also improve customer convenience.

Banks should choose the right design for a good customer experience from among the following:

- **Specialized counters:** Different counters to approach the tellers, open new accounts, for cards etc., so that customers can be serviced by staff specialized in that area. However, the customer has to be directed to the right counter depending on the service required.

- **Single-window:** A single window for all the services that a customer needs offers a much better customer experience but then care needs to be taken to ensure that the staff will be able assist the customer over a wide range of needs.

- **Optimized branch staff:** Staff with the right product expertise and in the right number will be required to offer faster service to customers. As the needs and the profile of the customers will continue to change over time, branch staffing needs to be optimized accordingly.

- **Product mix:** All branches offer basic services for accounts, deposits and payments. However, expertise is required to offer services for products like home loans, insurance, auto finance, foreign exchange etc. Banks may include those services only in relevant and large branches by staffing appropriate product experts.

- **Usage of technology:** Banks can take advantage of innovative use of technology to offer better service to customers at the branches. Some examples are mentioned below:

  - **Moving non customer facing activities to centralized operations:** Branches can be designed to be predominantly customer facing sales and marketing units and all the internal processing can be moved to a centralized processing unit. This will enable branch staff to spend more time with the customers to understand their needs. Also performing the operations from a low cost and centralized location will help reduce costs and achieve economies of scale. Electronic scanning and transmission of documents associated with customer records as well as workflow systems to track each work item will be key technology enablers to achieve this.

- **Virtual branch for special products:** Use of advance audio/video rooms in branches helps customers to be serviced by a centrally located specialist team for specialized products like home loans, insurance and investments. However, basic transactions can be serviced at the branch itself. This will enable banks to pool in their specialist resources and achieve economies of scale without compromising on customer experience. Some banks are experimenting with complete virtual branches to offer a comprehensive range of services.

Increasingly, branches are being seen as sales and customer contact offices. Time consuming non customer facing processes are being moved to centralized operations centres due to the following reasons:

- **Better utilization of resources due to economies of scale:** Also effective utilization of specialist resources in a centralized location instead of distributing them across branches.

- **Better enforcement of processes and compliance:** As the operations team does not have any direct interaction with the customers, processes can be enforced strictly and in a standardized manner. This will improve the bank's operations risk management capability.

Automatic Teller Machines (ATMs)

A large ATM network distributed across key locations is a major differentiator for a retail bank. It offers unmatched convenience, like 24x7 access by customers, low cost operations and brand promotion for the bank. Some of the ATM design considerations for a bank are described below:

- **Ownership:** Banks will typically use one of the following methods to set up ATMs:
  - **Own ATMs:** Banks will lease the space, set up the ATM, manage the ATM's availability and enter into an arrangement with third parties for physically handling the cash. Typically in-branch ATMs are owned and managed by the banks.
  - **Third party services:** Independent third party services can be used to provide white labelled ATM services branded in the

bank's name. Depending on the agreement, service providers lease the space, provide the ATM technology, manage cash arrangements and charge the bank on a transaction basis.

- **Agreement with a network of banks:** Banks can enter into an agreement with a network of banks to enable their customers to use the ATMs of any bank within the network. This provides a much wider ATM network coverage to its customers compared to its own network.

- **Network membership:** Banks will need to have membership of multiple payment card schemes like MasterCard, Visa or any regional or national payment network (e.g., RuPay in India). This will enable them to accept all the cards issued on any of these schemes. One can see a list of card schemes that are accepted at an ATM posted near the ATM machine itself. By having wider card scheme membership, banks will be able to accept the cards issued on those schemes at their ATMs, Merchant POS or online gateways irrespective of who the card holder is or which bank issued it.

- **Location:** Location of the ATMs can be in-branch or stand alone.

  - **In-branch ATMs:** There are a number of advantages to having in-branch ATMs, such as availability of space, network and security and they also help customers to carry out basic transactions themselves.

  - **Stand alone ATMs:** A number of arrangements have to be made for stand alone ATMs, like leasing space, security, and network connectivity to the bank's data centre. Stand alone ATMs are predominantly located for the convenience of customers in densely populated residential and business areas.

Corporate Office/Regional Offices

Corporate office/Regional offices are mainly for housing corporate staff like senior executives; heads of marketing, finance, HR and business managers etc. This is where the key decisions relating to a bank's strategic direction, product strategy, brand building, marketing campaigns, credit policies, regulatory interface and compliance etc., are taken. These offices are located in prime areas of major cities so that industry partners, high profile customers, regulators or auditors can access them easily.

These offices need to be connected to the bank's data centre to enable access to key enterprise applications like management reports, finance, HR, credit etc. Typically, management reports and dashboards are created from various applications for senior management on a daily basis. Operational staff accesses the various underlying applications to conduct their day to day activities.

Central Operations Centre

Corporate/Regional offices, branches and ATMs are mainly located in prime areas with convenient access to customers and different stakeholders. They are generally small facilities distributed across cities and towns within easy customer reach. However, the central operations centre is designed to consolidate the non-customer facing activities across the bank's branches located in different regions into a centralized location or just a few locations. Some of the key advantages of a centralized operations centre are:

- Pooling of staff and resources at a central location will improve utilization of resources and hence save costs.
- Reduction of real estate costs as operations centres need not be located in prime areas.
- Branch staff has more time to focus on customer needs and predominantly function as sales offices leaving most of the customer service functions to the operations centre.
- Back-office processes across the bank can be standardized by centralizing the processes. This offers more opportunities for improvement in processes and better compliance thus reducing operational risks.

There are different kinds of operation centres, which may be operating from different locations for various reasons. Some of the key operational functions are highlighted below:

- **Call centre operations:** Telephone banking/Call centre is one of the low cost customer servicing platforms for banks for basic non-cash service requests. This platform combines the advantage of direct customer interaction over the phone with centralized low cost operations. Call centre operations can be of two types:

- **Incoming call centre:** The customer will be able to reach out to the bank with service related requests like ordering a cheque book, requesting a duplicate statement, queries related to monthly instalments on home loans etc. Incoming call centre staff will first try to resolve the request/problem based on pre-documented steps for most commonly occurring scenarios. In case this is not feasible, they will capture a service request and route it to an expert team for further contact with the customer and resolution of the problem.

- **Outgoing call centre:** An outgoing call centre is mainly aimed at reaching out to different customers and prospective customers from a centralized location. Outgoing call centres can support various functions like informing prospects about promotional offerings, cross-sell to existing customers, follow up with customers on documentation and payment collections etc.

- **Payments processing centre:** This centre performs the back-office functions required for processing payments like processing cheques and manual actions required in processing electronic payments. Processing cheques can be of two types:

  - **Incoming cheques:** Cheques submitted by a bank's customers for credit into their accounts. These cheques may have been issued by another customer of the bank or an account holder of another bank. The operations team will sort incoming cheques based on the bank which has issued them. All the cheques issued by its customers, will be processed and debits/credits will be posted immediately. However, cheques from other banks will be sorted and routed to a regional/national cheque clearing system either physically or electronically. A customer will typically be credited once the cheque is cleared.

  - **Outgoing cheques:** Cheques written by their customers but deposited in other banks for collection. These cheques will come for clearing from a regional/national cheque clearing facility. In such cases, the operations team needs to validate the signature, check the balance, debit the customer's account, clear the cheque and confirm back to the regional/national cheque clearing system.

Cheque processing volumes are coming down rapidly but are still high. Handling electronic payments is much more efficient, cost effective and robust.

- **Back-office operations:** There are various back-office functions that are typically performed from a centralized operations centre. Some examples are:
  - **Printing and mailers:** Printing and sending of statements, promotional material, tax statements, PIN codes etc.
  - **Card personalization:** Personalization of debit/credit cards with account and security information, embossing the cards and mailing them to customers.
  - **Service requests:** Processing service requests received through the internet/telephone/ATM/branch, such as requests for a cheque book, change of address etc.
  - **Origination:** Processing of requests for a new credit card/ account/home loan/personal loan etc.
- **IT operations centre:** The key function of this centre is to ensure that various infrastructure, application and technical components of the bank are running smoothly. Some of the key elements of the IT operations centre are:
  - **Service desk:** This comprises a central team to assist various bank staff with any issues with bank IT applications. The service desk can typically be reached by multiple modes including telephone, e-mail, chat etc. The service desk is accessible only to bank employees facing IT system issues in serving customers. Service desk staff will try and resolve the issues based on a set of pre-documented procedures, e.g., password reset, account lockout etc. In case they are not able to solve the problem, they will capture the problem in a ticketing system and pass it on to an expert team. The service desk is responsible for tracking the ticket to closure

and informing the concerned bank employee who reported the problem.

- **Infrastructure support team:**   The infrastructure support team comprises specialists in various processor, storage and network solutions deployed in the bank data centre. This team will look at any reported problem in the area of infrastructure like the server not being available, data base sized being exceeded etc. Depending on the experience level, this team is divided into L1 and L2. L1 team will look into resolving issues based on set procedures whereas L2 team has more specialized skills necessary to resolve complex infrastructure problems. Usually there are a number of monitoring tools deployed to proactively track any potential problem before it occurs.

- **Application support team:**   A bank's application support team consists of people who are specialized in various products and customer built solutions deployed in the bank's environment. This team will try and resolve any application problems reported through the service desk. Usually a workaround will be attempted to resolve the issue and in case this is not possible a temporary fix by modifying the code or data will be deployed to restore the normal operation of the system. Further to restoration of normal system behaviour, the problem will be passed on to the application team for a permanent solution, if necessary.

- **Network Operations Centre (NOC):**   This team monitors the various networks of the bank connecting ATMs, branches, corporate/regional offices and processing centres. This team raises alerts in case of any potential threats or capacity issues foreseen.

- **Security Operations Centre (SOC):**   With the centralization of processing and account balances using core banking solutions, data becomes the most valuable asset for a bank. It is of utmost importance for a bank to ensure that its information assets are protected from information security threats. SOC is responsible for ensuring that security risks are properly mitigated.

It is not uncommon for banks to outsource IT operations either partially or completely. Also, there can be multiple partners providing IT operations for different areas of business. In such cases, access to a bank's data centres needs to be extended to the IT partners in a secured manner.

Data Centre

A data centre is one of the major investments for a bank and also a critical component of the bank's infrastructure. A data centre is where all the servers running the bank's applications are hosted in a secured manner and connected to all the other facilities like branches, ATMs, corporate/regional offices and operations centre via a wide area network. One of the critical requirements for data centres is business continuity, which means that in the case of any natural or man-made disruptions to the normal functioning of the primary data centre; technical operations should be shifted to a back-up data centre. To be able to achieve this, Disaster Recovery (DR) infrastructure should be similar to that of the primary data centre and data should be replicated from the primary data centre in near real-time.

For large global banks, there may be multiple data centres across different geographies with applications from that region hosted in that data centre. In such cases banks will be able to rely on other data centres in case of failure of one data centre. However, small banks may consider the services of a third party data centre provider for hosting their applications or providing disaster recovery or both.

APPLICATION LANDSCAPE

Retail banks typically have a complex set of applications to cater to the needs of the various stakeholders and infrastructure described above. In this section, we will look at the application landscape for automated banking operations. Figure 2.2 presents a simplistic overview of the application landscape of a bank.

Bank applications can be grouped under four heads.

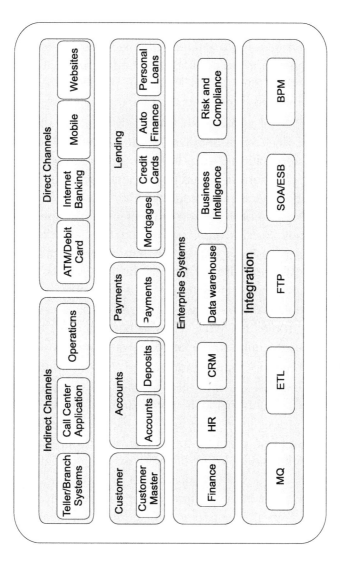

Fig. 2.2 *Application Architecture*

Channels

Channel applications provide access to various banking services for retail customers as well as bank staff servicing those customers. Channels can be viewed as a window to reach core applications like customer records, accounts, credit cards etc. Channel applications are broadly classified into indirect channels and customer channels. Indirect channels are the applications used by bank staff to support customers in their transactions. Customer channels are used directly by the customers to query and transact their accounts.

Indirect channel applications consist of branch staff applications, customer service representative applications (call centres), and operations applications etc. Indirect channel applications are aggregator applications designed for efficiently accessing the customer information for servicing the requests either in a branch, a call centre or from an operations centre. Indirect channel applications can be quite handy for the bank staff when they are designed based on a particular business transaction and aggregate all the relevant information. Allowing all user actions for that process from a single screen with minimum navigation, will significantly reduce the time taken to complete the business process. Also, built-in workflow that automatically routes the work items to bank staff depending on the business process until completion helps efficient tracking.

Customer channel applications like ATMs, internet banking, mobile banking and websites, allow customers to inquire about and operate their accounts/products. For customers, channel applications are meant for convenient and anytime access for banking services. Banks can use these channels to provide better user experience, and promote branding and relevant offers for existing customers. Customer channels are the cost efficient way of servicing once adaptation crosses a particular level. Customer channel applications have to be designed for high transaction volumes, 24x7 like availability, faster response times, and intuitive user interface for achieving higher adaptation.

Product Systems

Product systems maintain the core business data like customer records, accounts, deposits and loans etc. Product systems form the single factual source for all active customers and their account balances. There are different product systems for different products like accounts, loans, credit cards, payments etc. These product systems encompass complex business rules like interest computation, tax computation and authorization etc., to service them. There are many vendors who offer standard software packages for these individual products or a suite of software packages called 'core banking', covering a wide range of retail products. Processing credit cards is one of the most standardized offerings across banks worldwide, predominantly due to the fact that card processing is dominated by a few card schemes offering global operations. Due to the standardized nature of processing, there are large technology players offering credit card processing as a platform for banks. This service includes the software package, infrastructure and operations. There are also platform based offerings available from vendors for other products like mortgages at the national/regional level.

Enterprise Systems

Enterprise systems enable a bank's internal functions like marketing, finance, risk, HR and legal operations to perform the necessary functions. These applications enable a bank to operate smoothly, manage risk, manage its human resources, manage its assets, prepare financial statements, conduct campaigns etc. Across the industries, enterprise systems have been standardized in the form of ERP solutions from major technology players. These ERP solutions have industry specific versions considering the nuances of the industry, legal and regulatory requirements. For the banking industry, the criticality and importance of finance and risk systems is paramount and their enterprise systems are dominated by ERP solutions. However configuring the ERP solutions and building the interfaces with various product systems is a complex exercise considering the large number of business rules and interfaces.

Integration

Channels, products and enterprise systems need to be closely integrated to make automated banking processes work. The integration function handles the application, data and process integration functions across the various applications mentioned above, to offer comprehensive functionalities.

Application integration covers the real time interfaces between the applications. For example, the function of opening an account invoking the 'customer master application' to validate the existence of a customer already in the data base.

Data integration covers data flow, data validation and aggregation between applications. For example product systems like accounts, mortgage and credit cards, that send the data feeds to finance application for processing.

Process integration covers the integration of the various business processes to provide a comprehensive business service. For example, the loan origination process that invokes various processes from different internal/external systems to check the eligibility, credit rating and invoke approvals in an orchestrated manner to arrive at a decision.

These application groups are dealt with in more detail in subsequent chapters. Chapter 3 discusses indirect channel applications; Chapter 4 deals with customer channel applications; Chapter 5 discusses customer master applications; Chapter 6 deals with account/deposit applications; Chapter 7 deals with lending applications; Chapter 8 discusses payment applications; Chapter 9 discusses enterprise systems applications; Chapter 10 discusses integration applications; Chapter 11 discusses transformation programs and Chapter 12 takes care of off-the-shelf product options.

Each application architecture has been captured in diagrammatic format with the convention described in Figure 2.3.

Actors: Individuals/Organizations that use the applications

Applications: Applications/Components that perform the processing

Interfaces: Interfacing applications/components

Key data: Key data entities that are maintained in this application

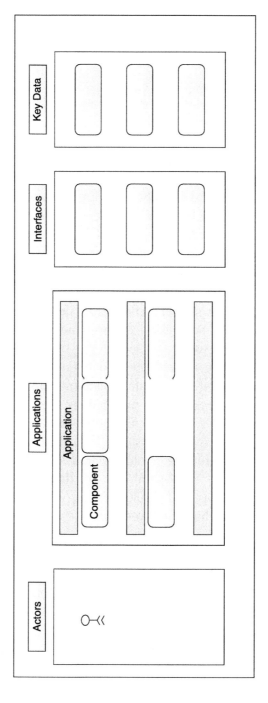

Fig. 2.3 *Application Architecture Template*

CHAPTER 3

Indirect Channels

Channels are the gateway for customers and bank staff to access the various services offered by product systems like accounts, deposits, credit cards and lending etc. Channel applications can be categorized as direct customer channels like ATMs, internet banking, mobile banking etc., and indirect channels like branches, call centres, operations etc. Customer channel applications are used by end customers to perform transactions independently without any support from bank staff. Indirect channel applications are used by bank staff or its representatives to offer various services to its customers. Banks would like to increase the usage of direct channels for commoditized transactions to reduce the overall cost and increase scalability.

Typically, branch staff/call centre staff need to access information from several applications like accounts, cards, lending etc., to service the needs of the customer. One of the options for the staff is to access and navigate through these different applications, search for the customer and retrieve/update the information as needed. This has the major disadvantage of low productivity and slower service to the customer, as branch staff or call centre operators have to navigate through screens of multiple systems. Usually, these product systems are based on different technologies that look and run completely differently with no interoperability. As the time taken to service the customer increases, it results in long wait times, low customer satisfaction and higher employee costs per transaction.

To address these issues, indirect channel applications like branch and call centre applications are mainly built as aggregator applications which combine the services/functions of multiple product systems with a business transaction view and efficient screen navigation. Process and navigation for indirect channels should be designed in such a way that the time taken to complete a transaction is kept to a minimum and also continuously optimized based on changing patterns of customer profiles and channel usage.

Bank's product systems need to expose their core product features as reusable services using which an integrated branch application or call centre application can be built. These applications will have customized navigations built according to the service catalogue of these functions. Also, these applications will have additional productivity features like telephone integration for call centres, cash register and reconciliation for branches etc.

Service Oriented Architecture (SOA) has been a significant enabler for a bank's staff to move away from working with legacy screens of various product applications to an aggregated, customer transaction driven, graphical user interface. SOA enables various stand alone functions of core product systems to be exposed as services using which stand alone applications can be built. Key themes under SOA that are essential for building aggregator applications are given below:

- Exposing existing functionalities from product systems as services, e.g., checking the account balance, retrieving customer records, or updating customer contact details etc.
- Publishing the service with a clear definition of service description, inputs and expected results. Teams handling channel development should be able to identify, with no ambiguity, which service is needed to be invoked, what information is required to be passed on and what is the format of the expected result.
- Authorization and authentication approach to validate the requests.

Indirect channels are broadly categorized into the following three classes.

- **Branch systems:** Applications which are available to branch staff to service customers visiting the branches. These applications provide teller as well as sales and service functionalities by interfacing with various product systems.
- **Call centres:** These applications are used in remote call centres to handle customer queries/service requests over the phone. These applications need to group the necessary information from various core product systems to support efficient servicing of customers' calls. Also, an efficient navigation mechanism

to support multiple product queries and registration of service requests is necessary.

- **Operations:** The operations team performs a number of back office processes that do not require direct/indirect customer connect, like processing payments, addressing customer service requests, processing loan documents etc. Operations applications will provide efficient and workflow based access to all the core and support applications to conduct operations tasks.

The key features of indirect channel applications are:

- **Connectivity to multiple product applications:** As a customer may come up with service requests related to any/multiple products, these applications need to have efficient and real time connectivity to product systems/relevant data.

- **Channel specific applications:** Apart from the connectivity to product systems, each of the above indirect channels will have specific applications to cater to the needs of that channel. For example branch systems will have a 'cash register' to track the cash at the counter. Similarly, a call centre will have a telephone system to efficiently track and route the incoming calls to the next available operator.

- **Smooth and efficient navigation:** Efficiency and faster services are the key to indirect channels, as employee productivity and customer experience are adversely affected due to slow and inefficient systems. Hence for these applications, the screen interface needs to be designed efficiently with minimum navigation for the users.

These channels have been further explained in detail in the following sections.

BRANCH SYSTEMS

Let us briefly look at the technical infrastructure of a branch:

- **Network equipment:** A branch should be connected to the bank's data centre using a Wide Area Network (WAN). Network equipment needed to connect the branch to the data centre like routers and switches should be installed securely within the branch.

Table 3.1   Branch Systems – Snapshot

Actors	• Tellers and sales/service representatives at the branch will use these applications to serve customers/prospective customers visiting the branch.
Interfaces	• Branch applications interface with all the key product systems, customer master, CRM systems to retrieve and update data as required. • Sales and service applications also interface with origination systems and document management systems for processing applications.
Key data	• Branch applications maintain the transaction history, cash transaction logs, reconciliation reports etc., for all the branch transactions.

- **ATM:**   Typically all the branches have in-branch ATMs to enable self-service for basic transactions. The ATM machine along with the necessary equipment needs to be installed and connected to the bank's data centre through network equipment.

- **Branch server:**   The need for the branch server depends on the application landscape and especially deployment architecture of the branch application. Branch applications can be either hosted in a branch server or in the centralized data centre. It is beneficial to have a very thin branch infrastructure and have all the applications centrally hosted in the data centre as this will mean more efficient centralized monitoring and support.

- **Printers:**   Branches will need specialized printers for printing cheques, passbooks, banker's cheques etc. Print layout and stationery design have to be aligned to ensure proper printing.

- **Scanners:**   Branch staff can use the scanning solution to electronically send the documents for processing at a centralized operations centre. These documents can include loan application forms, service requests or cheques. Document management solutions typically enable storing and cataloguing of various documents either independently or integrated with business applications like a record/case management system. A document management solution along with a scanning solution will enable scanning of the physical documents and attaching them to the customer case directly. Scanning solutions may also be located in centralized operations centres in which case branch staff will send the physical forms directly to the centralized operations centre.

• **Card/PIN readers:** Customer authorization can be in the form of a card/PIN entered and card/PIN readers need to be installed accordingly.

Branch application deployment can be designed considering various parameters like performance, response times and maintainability. The possible options for deployment are described below.

In-branch Deployment

Branch applications can be deployed within the branch server with integration to product systems deployed in a centralized data centre along with the provision for storage of local data to improve the response times. Figure 3.1 depicts the in-branch deployment of the branch systems.

This approach has the advantage of faster response times, but each branch needs to be equipped with the appropriate infrastructure for hosting branch applications. There are overheads in maintaining the servers and applications at each branch. It is also a cumbersome exercise to distribute enhancements to branch applications across a vast branch network.

Data Centre Deployment

Branch applications can be hosted in a centralized data centre along with other product applications. This approach has the advantage of maintainability and easy deployment for any changes. Figure 3.2 depicts the data centre deployment of branch applications.

On the other hand, availability and response times for all branch applications depend on the network connectivity to the central data centre.

Figure 3.3 presents the key functionalities of a branch application.

The applications/components of branch systems are further explained below.

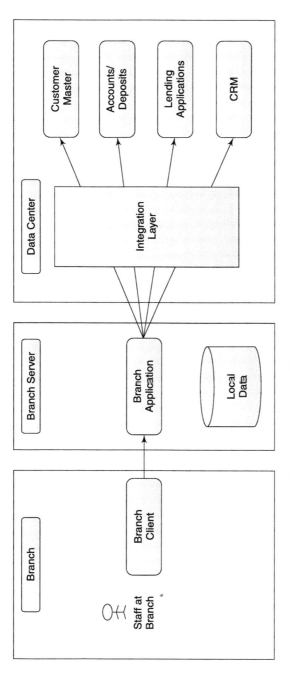

Fig. 3.1 *In-branch Development of Branch Systems*

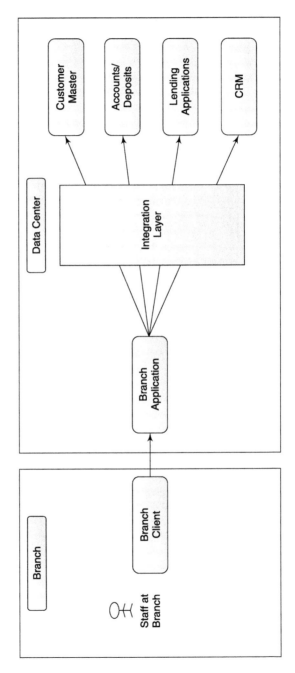

Fig. 3.2 *Data Center Deployment of Branch Systems*

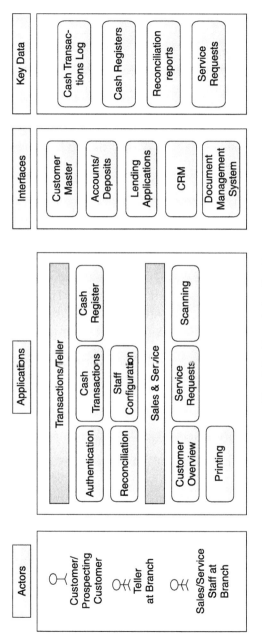

Fig. 3.3 *Branch Applications*

Transactions (Teller)

The key components necessary for handling cash transactions by a teller are:

- **Authentication:**   Customer authentication in most of the branches is done by verifying the signature or based on the card/PIN reader. In case of signature based verification, customer signatures are pre-scanned and associated with a customer's records electronically at the time of opening an account. A branch teller will be able to pull out the image of the customer's signature and compare it with the signature on the instruments submitted. In case of a card/PIN reader, the customer needs to swipe the card and enter the PIN. These details will be sent to the authentication server for validation. On successful authentication, the teller will be intimated about the same and the application will proceed to the next step.

- **Cash transactions:**   This application will enable branch tellers to capture and process cash transactions. This application will also interface to the corresponding product system to validate and post the transaction. Some examples of transactions are:
  - Depositing cash into a savings account
  - Closing a deposit and withdrawing the funds
  - Transfer of funds
  - FOREX transactions
  - Loading a pre-paid card

  As the above teller transactions map to different products, the corresponding product service needs to be invoked to validate and complete the transaction.

- **Cash register:**   The teller comes to his/her desk with the cash register with the initial inventory of cash. This is captured in the cash register system at the beginning of the day. During the day, every cash deposit/withdrawal is captured in the system including the denominations. So the cash register application will provide an effective mechanism to validate the cash in the box against the information available in the cash register system.

- **Reconciliation:** There are number of reconciliations performed to ensure that all the transactions are captured correctly. Cash register reconciliation will ensure that the cash in the box matches with the transactions.

- **Staff configuration:** Information about the branch staff and their authorization levels should be configured in the branch systems. All the transactions performed will be validated against the user's authorization levels. Additionally the supervisor's authorization will be required for certain transactions.

Sales and Service

Increasingly branches are being designed as customer contact and sales centres. There need to be appropriate IT systems to cater to the requirements of the sales and service staff at branches. The key components of this application are:

- **Customer overview:** This application should provide a comprehensive overview of customer information including the products currently used by the customer, recent contact history, service requests, potential options for cross-selling generated by analytics systems etc. Using this information, bank staff will be able to offer appropriate assistance and recommend suitable and relevant new products. This component leverages underlying product systems for customer master, Customer Relationship Management (CRM) and analytics.

- **Service requests:** Using this application, bank staff will be able to capture the service requests of customers. Service requests can be raised on any product; some examples are a complaint on a credit card transaction, submission of KYC documents, change of personal details like address, request for a cheque book etc. Bank staff will also collect the appropriate documents from a customer, such as proof of address for a change of address if necessary. These documents will be scanned and attached to the service request electronically. These service requests are usually processed by a centralized operations team and this team can access the service requests and the attached documents electronically. For service requests, this functionality is typically provided by interfacing with CRM applications and the document management system is interfaced with a scanning application.

- **Scanning:** The scanning application will enable the bank staff to electronically attach supporting documents to customer records in the system. This will enable remote servicing of these requests as well as keeping the electronic copy for easy storage and retrieval. Branch staff will also be able to accept application forms and relevant documents for new products like opening accounts, cards, loans etc. These documents along with the application forms will be scanned and captured in the system electronically. Scanning may also be centralized at the operations centre. These applications will be picked by the product origination team for various checks and on-boarding.

- **Printing:** There are various special printing needs at a branch like printing banker's cheques, demand drafts, statements, passbooks etc. Printing formats have to be aligned to the particular transaction and stationery. The printing application enables these features from various functions within the branch application. However bulk printing of statements and letters is usually generated and dispatched from the mailing room in operations.

CALL CENTRE APPLICATIONS

A call centre is a convenient channel for customers to access banking services for basic non-cash transactions/service requests. Call centre services can be availed of from any location and are usually available for a much larger time window than typical branch operation timings.

Call centre operations enable much better utilization of human resources for banks due to the fact that they constitute a centralized platform as compared to a distributed branch network. Call centre operations are typically performed from low cost, non-prime locations. Due to the above reasons, a call centre is also a much cheaper option for banks to service customers compared to the same services being offered at a branch.

Table 3.2 Call Centre Applications - Snapshot

Actors	• Call centre operators and management staff access these applications to serve customers reaching out to call centres.
Interfaces	• Call centre applications interfaces with CRM, customer master and all product systems.
Key data	Key data generated by call centre applications are: - customer call records, operator notes summarizing the calls and audit logs of manual actions performed by operators.

Call centre applications can be grouped under the following heads:

- **Incoming call centre:**   These applications help to service the customers reaching out to a bank for a query/service request.

- **Outgoing call centre:**   These applications help call centre agents to reach out to customers for purposes like new offers, follow-ups, collections etc.

- **Analytics:**   These applications provide the necessary intelligence like call volumes, product wise call volumes, queue depths, average call times, waiting times and call drop rates at various times during the day. This will help an operations manager refine call centre operations, such as shifts, number of employees per shift etc.

Figure 3.4 presents an overview of call centre applications.

Applications/Components of call centre systems are further explained below.

Incoming Call Centre

- **Interactive Voice Response (IVR):**   The interactive voice response application acts as the first point of contact for a customer reaching out to a call centre. IVR applications typically perform the following functions:

  - **Customer authentication:**   IVR applications attempt to authenticate the customer in an automated fashion by requesting customer identification and authorization codes like PIN/telebanking PIN etc.

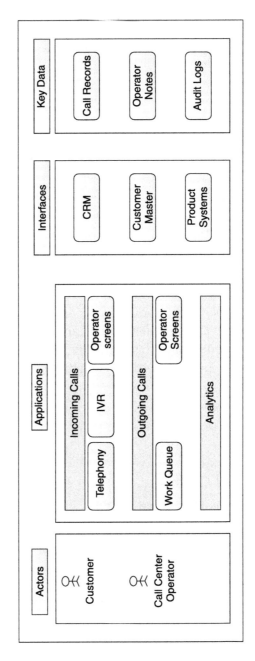

Fig. 3.4 *Call Center Applications*

- **Basic transactions:** Some of the service requests can be completely automated by IVR without any need for intervention by a call centre operator. The customer is given list of options to choose from and the phone dial-pad is used to select the option. Some examples of these transactions are checking the account balance, last five transactions, credit card balance, ordering a cheque book etc. Basic transactions in an automated fashion are possible only if the customer is able to provide authentication information within the IVR application. The Computer Telephony Integration (CTI) component will be leveraged by the IVR system to interface with the call centre application to process these transactions.

- **Data collection:** IVR is also used to reduce the effective time required for the call centre operator to service the request by pre-collecting data. An IVR system can collect basic information about the customer, like the account number, service required and possible authentication. This information will be used in two ways. One is to route it to the right team within the call centre based on the customer classification and the service requested. Second, all the information captured will be routed from the IVR system to the call centre application to retrieve the customer information on the screen by the time the agent is on the phone with the customer. This will save a significant amount of time for each call. The agent will have to authenticate the customer if it is not done via the IVR system by asking a few questions about past transaction details etc.

- **Telephony:** The basic technology for a call centre is a good telephony solution that can receive multiple telephone calls, queue them and route them through to the available operators in a queue. It is important for the telephony system to provide good statistical information like average call time, average waiting time, call dropout rates over a period of time during the day and also across the days in a week.

- **Call centre application (Operator screens):** A call centre application is used by operators to service customers. As discussed earlier, this application will typically be interfaced with IVR to pre-fill incoming customer details. Operators will be able to authenticate customers using this application, if it has not been done earlier in the IVR application. Operator screens have to be designed keeping in mind the service catalogue of the call centre and the most efficient way of handling those requests so as to reduce the time per call.

The call centre application invokes the underlying services offered by core products applications to show the necessary information. In this application, screens will aggregate data from multiple applications to be able to serve the customer effectively, for example credit card balance, out-standing loan amount and savings account balance may be shown on one screen. The call centre application also interfaces with the CRM application for retrieving service request history or for capturing a fresh service request. All the customer call records along with operator notes and resolution will be logged and a history will be maintained.

Outgoing Call Centre

An outgoing call centre is predominantly meant for calls initiated by bank staff/agents to connect with the customers, for example, follow-up with customers on KYC documentation, calls for cross selling or as part of the collections process for outstanding payments.

An outgoing call centre will have application components for work queue and operator screens.

- **Work queue:** Depending on the outgoing call service, underlying data from product systems (like customer master for KYC follow-up, CRM for cross sell opportunities or collection system for payment follow-up) will be fed into the work queue system. These data include customer details, contact information and any other information related to the outgoing call. The work queue system is tightly integrated with the telephony system and will route the work items to the available operators.
- **Call centre application (Operator screens):** Operator screens will depend on the business process supported. The work queue application will pass the customer's data and all relevant details to this application. These details will be shown on the screen of

the operator who has been assigned the task. The operator will be able to look at the details and dial the customer's number manually or at the click of a button. The operator will also be able to capture a summary of the interaction with the customer for future reference. Some of this revised information may be sent back to the product systems (CRM, collections etc.,) for updating records.

Consider the collections process for example. The collections application will pick up all the borrowers who have defaulted on payments beyond a certain date. It will also shortlist the customers that need to be followed-up through telephone calls using collection strategy rules. These records with the required data like customer details, total outstanding, number of days since the payment was due, last follow-up call made etc., will be sent to the work queue application for processing in the outgoing call centre.

The workflow system routes these records to an available collections operator. On receiving the record on screen, the agent will be able to dial the customer and discuss the overdue payment. At the end of the call, the operator will capture the remarks about the call in the system and move on to the next record pushed to the screen by the workflow system. These updated records will be pushed back into the collections system for processing and updates to the collections data.

Analytics

It is important for the operations managers and senior management to have comprehensive information about the call centre operations for tactical planning needs like planning shifts, resource planning, training needs etc., as well as strategic planning needs like planning the work force, future expansion projections and channel strategy. The incoming call centre provides data like average call time, average waiting time, call dropout rates, customer profile, product, time of the day, week of the month, etc. Similarly, the outgoing call centre provides data like service, work queue depth, average call times, daily target vs. actual, customer profile etc. The analytics application will process these data and present them in the form of configurable management reports from various perspectives for both operational and senior managers.

In summary, the characteristics of a good call centre application are:

- Well-designed, user friendly screens tailored for business transactions
- Efficient integration with product systems
- Telephony solution that helps reduce an operator's time needed for the call
- Analytics that help the bank to plan the operations

CHAPTER 4

Customer Channels

In the early days, a branch was the only option for customers to interact with the bank and transact on their accounts. However, technology has provided new channels for customers to access the banking services directly without any assistance from the bank's staff. These channels provide unmatched convenience to customers as well as cost efficiencies and scalability to the bank. ATMs/Debit cards, internet banking and mobile banking are the main customer channels offered by banks. There are some key differences between the technology requirements for indirect channels and customer channels as given below:

- Indirect channels like a branch or a call centre have specified operating hours and availability requirements of these applications is limited to the operating hours. However customer channels should be available nearly $24 \times 7 \times 365$ and any downtime will cause significant inconvenience to customers.

- Indirect channel applications are used only by bank staff/contractors and users will be in the range of hundreds or thousands. Customer channel applications are used by a large customer base that could be in millions. So it is important for customer channels to support large transaction volumes and provide acceptable response times to user requests.

- Indirect channels are accessed from secured locations like a branch or a call centre where banks can deploy several additional security measures. However customer channels are accessed from anywhere and hence strong digital security measures should be put in place.

- Indirect channels are used by trained staff and hence are designed to offer maximum functionality with an aim to process a transaction in the shortest possible time. However in case of customer channels, interface design needs to be simple, intuitive and user friendly to cater to the diverse customer base.

In this chapter, we will discuss the technology supporting ATM, internet banking, mobile banking and website services.

ATM/DEBIT CARD

The ATM was the first self-service channel using which customers were able to query and transact independently on their accounts. Over time, ATMs became more sophisticated, acting as mini-branches offering almost all the services of a branch but without the branch staff. A wide ATM network helps to provide convenient access to customers and also promotes the brand. Banks also accept and subscribe to a wide range of card schemes like VISA, MasterCard etc., and generate some revenue from ATM usage by customers of other banks.

Some options for banks to offer a wider ATM network for their customers are given below:

- Banks can establish their own ATMs either in-branch or at convenient prime locations including leasing of space, ATM equipment, in-house/third party arrangements for physical cash etc. In this option, banks can connect their ATMs with multiple card schemes so as to be able to accept a wider range of cards.

- Outsourcing the setting up and management of ATMs to a third party as a white-labelled service but still branded in the bank's name.

- Banks can also issue debit cards associated with a card scheme so that customers can use a wider ATM network, and are not restricted only to their own bank. Banks may have tie-ups with other banks to offer free usage of their ATMs. Banks may also be able to divert their customers to use their debit cards at point-of-sale devices at merchant locations or using payment gateways online instead of cash transactions. Electronic payment at merchant locations or online gateways using a debit card is preferred by banks over cash transactions at an ATM as none of the high cost elements like real estate, physical handling of cash are required in electronic transactions.

ATM/Point of Sale (POS) systems have the highest availability and response requirements. Complexity of the underlying infrastructure, processing and security are hidden under a simple and user friendly interface to customers.

Figure 4.1 presents an overview of ATM/POS applications.

An ATM consists of the components listed in Table 4.1.

Table 4.1   ATM/POS Applications - Snapshot

Actors	• These applications cater to customers transacting at a bank's ATMs or merchant POS terminals or online gateways by using an ATM/debit card issued on a particular card scheme.
Interfaces	• Customer master, product systems, card scheme network and independent cash provider systems are some of the key interfaces for this application.
Key data	• ATM/POS device information, plastic card information, authentication information, accounts and transaction information are the key data entities for this application.

Applications/Components of ATM/POS systems are further explained in the sections below.

Setup Management

The components under an ATM setup and management application are as follows:

- **ATM client software:**   This is deployed inside the ATM machine. ATM client software provides the necessary user screens for customers to conduct their transactions. The ATM client also connects with the transaction management server component in the data centre to authenticate and authorize transactions. An ATM client will have the encryption mechanism for PIN numbers before transmitting them over the network for authentication. ATM clients will also interface with various auxiliary devices in the ATM, such as a cash dispensing machine, cash counting machine, cheque scanner, receipt printer etc., to complete the transaction requested by the customer. As client software is installed across the entire ATM network, any new version of the client software has to be distributed in a timely manner.

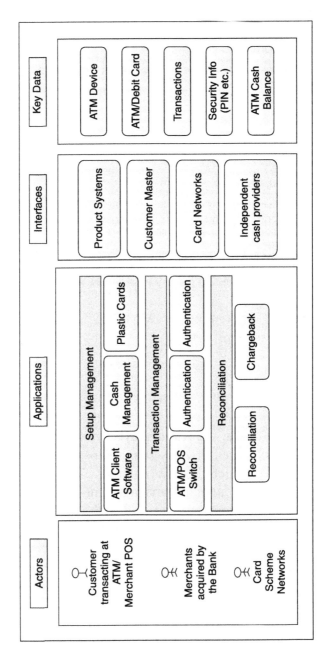

Fig. 4.1 *ATM/POS Applications*

- **Cash management:** This component is deployed in the bank's data centre and keeps track of the cash available in different ATMs. This software projects the cash requirements in different ATMs and places necessary instructions for cash refill. Typically, cash refill services are outsourced to 'independent cash management' firms and necessary instructions are sent to them automatically for cash refill. Once cash is loaded into ATMs, the information will be received automatically by this application to reflect the cash available in each ATM.

- **Plastic cards:** This component keeps track of the entire life cycle of the ATM/debit cards including issuance, personalization, lost/stolen cards, re-issuance after expiry date, PIN details for authentication and mapping to the account etc. This application will not have any account or transaction details on its own but the card details are linked to the customer's account in the core banking system. This application will have interfaces for card personalization and embossing devices to prepare the card and deliver it to the customer.

Transaction Management

The components under the transaction management application that caters to customers' transactions in an ATM are as follows:

- **ATM/POS switch:** This is a high performance application deployed to handle ATM/POS requests in a bank's data centre. All the requests from all the bank's ATMs and POS machines across the country/globe will be routed to the ATM/POS switch for appropriate routing and response. A request from an ATM machine for a transaction can be either from its own customers or someone using the card of a bank-subscribed card scheme. Similarly, a POS transaction from a merchant terminal acquired by the bank can be from one of its own customers or someone using the card of a bank-subscribed card scheme. An ATM/POS switch acts as a router between the bank's ATM/POS machines and the corresponding internal processing system or card scheme. An ATM/POS switch will route the incoming requests of the bank's own customers also called "on-us transactions" to internal systems, whereas other card transactions are routed to the corresponding card scheme network for authentication and authorization. The formats of data exchange with internal product systems and different card schemes are usually different and an ATM/POS switch manages the function of converting one format to other as needed to complete the transaction.

- **Authentication:** For cards issued by the bank, an ATM/POS switch routes the ATM transactions to internal systems for authentication and authorization. Authentication is the process of confirming the identity of the customer and is typically done using a secured PIN number associated with the ATM/debit card. As a first step in an ATM transaction, the customer is asked for authentication using the associated PIN number. The encrypted PIN number along with the card details will be routed to this component. The authentication component decrypts the PIN details received over the network and validates it against the card details. For debit card transactions at POS devices, authentication can be carried out manually in the form of a signature on the transaction slip or electronically by the PIN number entered by the customer. Electronic real time authentication enables real time transfer of funds at the point of sale, thus avoiding transaction slips and signatures. Electronic real time authentication also enables retailers to offer small cash withdrawals at the time of a transaction.

- **Authorization:** The authorization component performs the transaction validations and account balance checks necessary to authorize the transactions. Authorization is a high performance transaction service provided by the core banking product system. Once authorized, the necessary bookings will be posted to the account to reflect the revised balance in the account.

Reconciliation

The components under the reconciliation application are as follows:

- **Reconciliation:** Banks also need to carry out internal reconciliation everyday between ATM/POS transactions, cash balances and card scheme data to ensure that all financial transactions have been correctly captured and executed. This application manages the reconciliation process for ATM/POS transactions.

- **Chargeback:** The charge back mechanism handles the automatic credit of customer accounts for issues related to cash disbursement at ATMs. These are identified as part of reconciliation and necessary credits will take place.

INTERNET BANKING

Internet banking (also called online banking) is a secured online application that allows customers to access their accounts from anywhere using a computer with internet connectivity. Customers are willing to spend more time on internet banking as compared to the time they spend in a branch or in front of an ATM. This gives banks a big opportunity to offer more advanced banking features to customers like bill payments, standing instructions and transfer of funds as well as to promote the relevant and customized products and offers. The internet banking application should not be seen just as a front-end for product systems but as an integrated customer facing banking application that offers comprehensive banking services with rich customer experience and high performance.

Some of the key features of an internet banking application are described below.

- An internet banking platform needs to be highly scalable (to handle large volumes of concurrent users), highly available (potentially 24x7) and highly secure (multiple levels of security).

- Internet banking is not just another channel to access core products. It is an independent banking application that offers comprehensive banking services (accounts, cards, mortgages etc.), rich and user-friendly features for self-service, access to various customer service requests etc.

- An internet banking application interfaces with core product systems for data access and updates. To manage scalability, a large part of the data is available locally within the internet banking application by way of replication. There will, however be

Table 4.2 Internet Banking Applications-Snapshot

Actors	An internet banking application is used by customers to access banking services from anywhere. This application is also used by the administration team for configuration, like user access, billings etc.
Interfaces	Key interfacing applications for internet banking are customer master, product systems like accounts, credit cards, lending etc., payments and CRM applications.
Key data	Apart from the replicated data, internet banking will maintain application specific information like biller details, bill payment requests, funds transfer instructions and alerts etc.

invocation of core product services for certain online transactions like the latest balance, posting of debits/credits etc.

Figure 4.2 represents the deployment view of an internet banking application. Internet banking is deployed as an independent application and will interface with other banking applications in both batch and real-time interface.

The key components of an internet banking application are described in Figure 4.3.

Internet banking consists of the following applications/ components:

Products

Typically internet banking provides a comprehensive view of all the products used by the customer with the ability to drill-down and view the details of each product.

- **Accounts:** Customers can view all their current accounts and access the balance, transaction history, statements etc.
- **Deposits:** Customers can view all the deposits, update instructions etc. A customer may also be able to open a fresh deposit or prematurely close a deposit, Such requests will be serviced by interfacing with the deposits application.
- **Cards:** This application will show all the cards used by the customer, transaction details, bill details etc. A customer will be able to pay his/her credit cards bill online and such requests will be serviced by interfacing with the payments application.

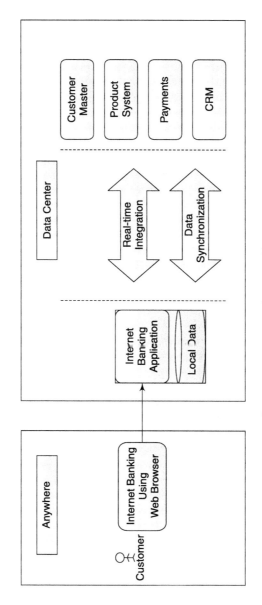

Fig. 4.2 *Internet Banking Deployment View*

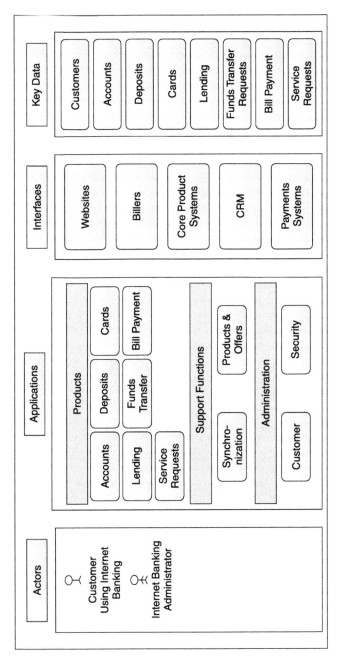

Fig. 4.3 *Internet Banking Applications*

- **Lending:** A customer will be able to view all the outstanding loans, current balance, due date of next payment etc. Customers will be able to generate reports corresponding to their loans.

- **Transfer of funds:** Customers will be able to capture the payees and initiate one-time or recurring requests for the transfer of funds. An internet banking application will interface with a payments application to service these requests.

- **Bill payments:** Using this application, customers will be able to register for specific billers and initiate one-time or recurring bill payments. Depending on the bill payment infrastructure available, banks may tie-up with a list of billers directly or with national bill payment infrastructure to enable a customer to pay the bill. The bill payment feature is dealt with in more detail in the section on 'Payments'.

- **Service requests:** Using the internet banking application, customers will be able to raise service requests like ordering cheque books, query transactions, order demand drafts/banker cheques etc. These service requests are captured into CRM systems and are serviced by back-office operations.

Support Functions

- **Synchronization:** As internet banking is accessed a great deal, all the key information like accounts, transactions, deposits etc., is typically replicated for faster customer response. There will be a periodic synchronization process to replicate the current transactions.

- **Products & offers:** This application helps promote the relevant products and offers to customers while they are using the internet banking applications. Depending on the bank's underlying analytics program, the relevance of the products and offers will vary. A comprehensive underlying analytics platform enables banks to offer very relevant offers and products to customers while using internet banking and improve the success rate in cross-selling.

Administration

- **Customers:** This application holds the list of customers and the eligibility for internet banking access.

- **Security:** Security is of utmost importance for internet banking and usually there are multiple lines of security, some of which are described below:
  - **https:** The first and simplest line of security is the usage of https protocol instead of http which will encrypt all the data exchanged between the browser and internet banking server. This will prevent possible attacks from persons listening to the network.
  - **Soft keypads:** Another feature of security is using soft keypads on screens to prevent someone from tapping the keyboards on computers in public places like kiosks.
  - **User id and password:** Each account is accessed through a unique user id and password which are supposed to be known only to the account owner.
  - **Transaction password:** This is an additional password for value transactions for additional security.
  - **Password grid:** A pre-dispatched password grid to the customer will enable additional authentication.
  - **SMS code:** For login or financial transactions, an SMS code can be used as an additional method to authenticate the identity of the user. In this case, the internet banking application will have the necessary interface with messaging utility.

MOBILE BANKING

Mobile banking extends the convenience of home banking to anywhere banking. Customers will be able to access banking services from anywhere at any time using their mobile phone. The mobile banking channel offers banks an additional opportunity to drive customers to self-service thus reducing the branch footfalls as well as reducing physical handling of cash. Reduced branch footfalls for basic transactions and reduced physical handling of cash will result in significant cost savings and improved operational efficiencies for the banks.

A mobile banking application is typically built as part of or on top of the internet banking solution. Recent advances in mobile technology with improved storage and processing speeds as well as improvements in mobile communication speeds have provided a number of technological opportunities to offer advanced mobile banking solutions.

Figure 4.4 presents the mobile banking technology options.

Outgoing SMS

An SMS alert is a feature provided as part of internet banking to set options for receiving SMS alerts. Customers will be able to set alerts on debits/credits to their accounts as well as on their credit cards. An SMS integrator will be used to send these messages to the registered mobile number of the customer.

Incoming SMS Based Banking

Initially, banks started offering some basic functions as part of mobile banking through SMS messages. Customers can send predefined codes from their registered mobile number to receive information like account balance, last transactions etc. However this service is not user friendly and only limited services can be offered as it is not interactive.

Mobile Friendly Internet Banking

Usually a mobile screen is much smaller compared to a desktop/laptop computer hence the needs of mobile users are different. Internet banking application screens are rich in information, however in the case of mobile phones customers expect limited information that is legible on small screens. Mobile friendly screens are designed keeping these considerations in mind, and appropriate screens are delivered depending on the connecting device.

Mobile Banking App

New mobile operating systems enable third party developers to build applications that can run on their operating systems like iOS, Android etc. Mobile applications provide a superior user interface as

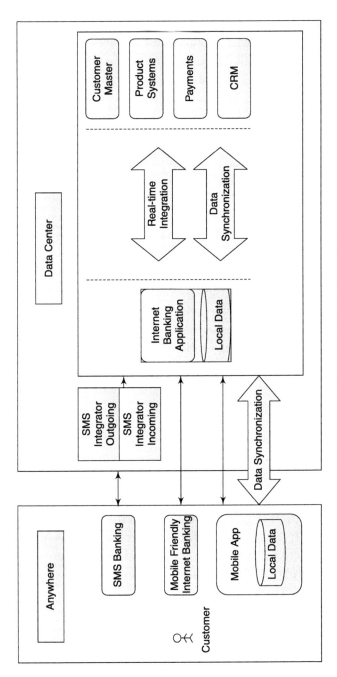

Fig. 4.4 *Mobile Banking Technology Options*

compared to mobile friendly internet banking, as there is a provision for storing the context and local data. A mobile application combines user experience of the client server model with the flexible access provided by thin client browser based applications. All enhancements to the mobile banking application can be distributed automatically or through an intuitive interface provided by an 'appstore.' Mobile banking applications need to be developed for multiple mobile operating systems like Apple, Android and Blackberry and also variants for mobiles and tablet computers. Mobile banking applications should also have local data storage of static data to improve the user experience.

In this chapter, we have discussed the mobile phone as a channel for accessing regular banking services. However there is lot of industry work in progress to use a mobile phone as an enabler for financial inclusion and payments. These topics are further discussed under the section 'Payments' in this book.

It is important for a bank to get its channel strategy right to achieve scalability and contain costs. A bank also needs to understand its customer profile and spend appropriate efforts on the relevant channels. Also, the right channel strategy could be a potential fee revenue earner, for example combining mobile banking with m-commerce could potentially lead to an income from additional fees.

WEBSITES

Websites are an effective marketing medium for banks to communicate with customers and prospects. A bank can promote its brand, describe its products and publish necessary documents like application forms etc. A well designed bank website with appealing graphics and faster response times can make a good impression on its visitors. Some of the effective uses of websites for banks are:

- Providing information to the various categories of customers, e.g., retail, business and corporate customers.
- Brochures to describe the various products offered.
- Publishing the latest information about interest rates, lending rates, FOREX rates etc.

- Providing self-help calculators for loan eligibility, monthly payments, maturity amount of a deposit, etc.
- Downloading application forms for new accounts, credit cards, home loans, etc.
- Capturing potential customers through "inquiry forms" to be filled in by customers for offline follow-up.
- Submitting application forms online for certain products. The KYC process may still happen offline.

The following factors are considered in designing the websites.

- **High volume of hits:** The capacity has to be designed considering the potentially large number of hits to the website, so that it is still able to respond within a reasonable time.
- **Security:** While there may not be major financial implications, a compromised website can harm the image of a bank. It is important for the bank to have absolute control on the content displayed on its website.
- **Content creation:** A website should always display the latest and most relevant information. This means a faster turnaround time for website updates. It is important for a business to have the flexibility to create content without heavily depending on IT.
- **Content management:** Websites should have the right internal control mechanisms to ensure that the content has gone through the appropriate guidelines for creation, review and editing before being published.
- **Statistical information:** An important feature of a website's component is to capture the number of visitors to various pages. This will enable them to understand the usage of this channel and also to refine the information displayed according to customers' interests.

Initially websites were created as a series of web pages and hosted on a web server by experienced programmers. However, marketing/business had to depend on the experienced programmers to make changes to their websites. This made it time consuming, error prone and effort intensive to change/enhance content. Web/ Electronic content management products aim to address this very

Table 4.3 Websites Applications-Snapshot

Actors	Website content is created and managed by a bank's marketing department and this information is accessed by customers/prospects to understand a bank's products. Website administration manages the configuration of the website, user access and analytics.
Interfaces	Websites usually offer links to internet banking as well as some relevant external sites.
Key data	• Website content like product information, marketing material, application forms etc. • Analytical information on the website usage.

issue and aim to give the control on content back to the business. Web/Electronic content management systems provide the tools for the business to create/modify the content, support the workflow needed for content approval and the run-time environment to deploy the content.

Figure 4.5 depicts the application architecture of a website application implemented on a content management product.

The key application components of a modern content management solution are described in the sections below.

Content Management

- **Configuration:** This component enables a website administrator to configure the website by defining the following factors:
  - Structure of the website.
  - Authorization and authentication details of the marketing staff's access to the website's application.
  - Workflow rules for various types of content.
  - Standards and templates.
- **Content editor:** This component allows the marketing staff or business users to create or modify the website content directly without any dependency on IT. Usually this application allows the user to capture the content exactly as it appears in the website, in predefined templates to enable a uniform look and feel. These changes have to be reviewed and approved before they can be made visible on the website.

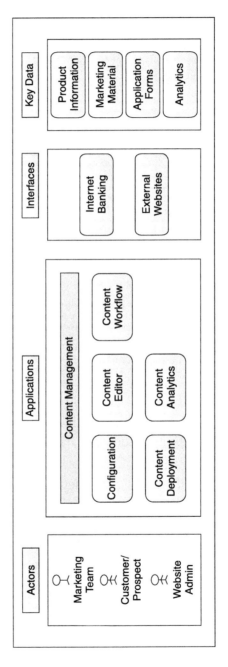

Fig. 4.5   *Websites Applications*

- **Content workflow:** Any changes to the content will be routed to the reviewer and approver as per the workflow configuration for the content. This is to ensure that the content is reviewed and verified at appropriate levels before being published.

- **Content deployment:** This is the run time component of the website's application to ensure that the website content is fully available. This component caters to the scalability, availability and performance of the website according to the business needs. All the authorized content will be pushed to the deployment instantly or at predefined times.

- **Content analytics:** This component collects detailed statistics of the various web pages and user actions. These reports will be used to refine the content of the website as well as to understand the customers' interests on information/products displayed on the website.

CHAPTER 5

Customer Master

Traditionally, banks have taken a product specific approach to their operations like customer acquisition, opening accounts and maintenance. Product systems are either commercially available solutions from different vendors or built in-house over a period of time and have their own customer data i.e., the credit card system contains the list of customers using the credit card products, the mortgage product maintains the list of customers using the mortgage product etc. Another reason that caused spreading of customer information across multiple systems was mergers and acquisitions. At the time of mergers and acquisitions, banks will have product systems and customer data from different entities coming together. Banks take up an integration program to consolidate the product systems and data to reduce the IT footprint and total cost of ownership. However some banks may choose to maintain multiple product systems and customer data, either due to a potential further sale or lack of business for full scale integration. This will also result in the bank's customer data being distributed in multiple product applications of different brands. Figure 5.1 gives a schematic overview of the product specific customer data.

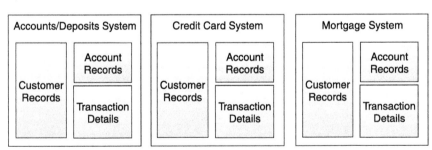

Fig. 5.1 *Product Specific Customer Data*

There is an increased realization that the cost of acquiring a new customer for a product is higher than selling the same to an existing customer. Customer retention, customer relationship management and customer mining have become important elements in a bank's growth strategy. Banks have started realigning towards a customer centric approach instead of a product centric approach. Single customer master is an important IT capability and will be a significant competitive differentiator.

Single customer master can provide the following benefits:

- **Customer experience:** Banks can provide a rich experience to the customer when they have a full view of the customer profile, all the products that the customer is using etc. This should help improve customer satisfaction and retention.

- **Improved success rate in cross-sell:** Single customer data and analytics around a customer profile helps banks to identify opportunities for selling additional relevant products to its customers. As these offers are highly targeted based on the customer profile, the success rate will be higher compared to a generic campaign.

- **Compliance:** All the regulatory requirements including KYC, data retention and data auditing can be better complied with, with the help of consolidated customer data.

- **Behavioural scoring:** As part of the risk management process, banks will be able to arrive at the behavioural scoring of customers based on their transactions across the products and get a better view of any potential default.

- **Product strategy:** Banks can analyze the product mix used by the customer base and make necessary changes to product strategy.

However, the real question is: How to build the single customer master?

The ideal, but not practical approach, would be to have one centralized customer master application for managing the customer data for the entire bank. All the new customer additions and modifications to existing customer data will be done in this system. Product applications across the bank refer to centralized customer data. This would mean a highly complex and scalable customer master application that can cater to the requirements of all products.

This approach is not practical for most banks, due to the following reasons:

- A large existing legacy application landscape will require huge investments to change all product systems to refer to centralized customer data.
- Bank applications consist of legacy product systems as well as off-the-shelf product systems which make it architecturally complex to carve out the customer master function.

An alternate non-intrusive approach is to build an independent centralized customer register from the customer data in different product systems. Key features of this approach are:

- An independent centralized customer register that contains unique customer records across all product systems.
- The customer register will contain the unique customer id as well as important customer details.
- The unique customer id in the centralized customer register will be linked with the customer ids of various product systems. Customer details will continue to be maintained within the individual product systems.
- Provision of a facility to update the customer register to link, de-link, re-link the unique customer id with the customer id from various product systems.
- Feature to capture relationships between different customers within the customer register. For example, the bank should be able to capture the relationships between its individual customers as well as between its individual and corporate customers.
- Sophisticated processing to synchronize the changes to customer data from various product systems into the centralized customer register. Further dissemination of this information to all relevant product systems, e.g., change of mobile number registered with card application to be marked in the central register and then propagated to a mortgage system.
- Centralized customer data to serve as the source for all the customer insights and intelligence.

Figure 5.2 provides a diagrammatic overview of the centralized customer register approach.

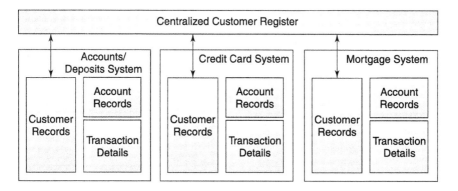

Fig. 5.2 *Centralized Customer Register*

Challenges in building a single customer master:

- Customer data are available in all the product systems. A single customer may be identified by a different, unique id in each system like deposits, loans, cards etc. These different records have to be intelligently identified as belonging to the same customer in the master.

- Discrepancies in data formats and values across different product systems, e.g., address formats, phone numbers etc.

- Master vs. slave: Once the single customer data is created and base-lined, any further changes to master data, like change of address are recorded and these changes are synchronized across different systems.

Diagrammatic representation of the centralized customer register and key data elements is presented in Figure 5.3.

Key data elements are described below:

- **Unique customer id:** This is a unique number for the customer across the bank, generated within the customer master application.

- **Customer identifier in the product systems:** In the customer register, each unique customer id is mapped to customer identifiers in different product systems. For example if a customer is using savings account and credit card services, the customer may be identified by different codes in these product systems.

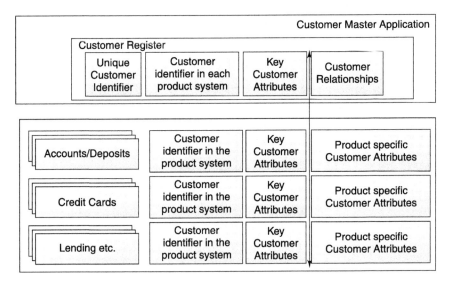

Fig. 5.3 *Centralized Customer Register*

The customer register will map these different ids to the unique customer id.

- **Key customer attributes:** The amount of key customer information stored as part of the customer register is dependent on the usage requirements of the data. At the minimum, data needed to uniquely identify the customer like national identification number, date of birth, telephone contact details, address etc., should be maintained. It is also preferable to keep the attributes that are to be queried or analyzed frequently in the centralized customer register for easy information retrieval. Otherwise, the query has to be performed across diverse systems, which can be performance intensive. Also, it is preferable to keep only those attributes that are relevant across the products in the customer register.

- **Customer relationships:** Relationships between the customers can be captured in the customer register, e.g., if a customer has a savings account and a mortgage and his spouse is using credit card services from the bank, it should be possible to link the two customer records within the customer register. This will give rich insights to the bank and help them improve the customers' experience and offer more tailored solutions to the customers based on their combined net worth.

Table 5.1   Customer Master Applications–Snapshot

Actors	Customer master information is predominantly useful to get a 360 degree view of the customer for sales, service and marketing staff. The data steward will access the customer master application to handle any exceptions in automatic processing of customer master records.
Interfaces	The customer master application will have interfaces with all the product systems for synchronization of customer records. Customer master will also feed data to CRM and data warehouse systems.
Key data	The customer master will maintain the customer register with unique customer id, key customer attributes, relationship with the product system identification and inter relationships between customers.

Figure 5.4 represents the key components of a customer master application. Customer records/updates from each product application in the pre-defined data format are extracted and fed to the customer master application for processing.

Key application components are described below.

Customer Register

- **Data quality checks:**   There are business rules to validate the quality of the customer data received from product systems, e.g., mandatory fields (like date of birth), value range for an attribute (like age), interdependencies (max value > minimum value etc.). Ideally these validations must have been performed on the source systems before the start of the data loaded to the customer master as part of data profiling. Only the records that pass through data quality checks will be pushed to the next stage, other records are set aside for exception processing.

- **Data de-duplication:**   It is possible that a customer record that is passed on from the product system already exists in the customer register captured from another product application. Data de-duplication is an intelligent search on the customer register based on unique customer attributes like national identification number, address and telephone number etc., to verify whether

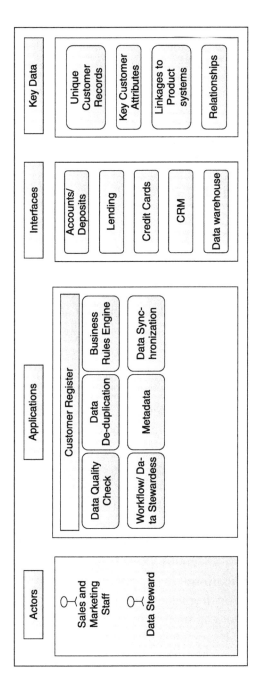

Fig. 5.4 *Customer Master Applications*

the record already exists. The outcome of data de-duplication matching is mentioned in terms of certainty. All records that match above a defined certainty level will be automatically considered as the same and the records will be merged. All records that match below a certainty level will be considered by the system as separate records. Anything in between will be routed for manual intervention and resolution. Also, when an incoming customer record from the product system is matched with an already existing customer record in the customer register, the system will overwrite or ignore or merge the records as per business rules defined.

- **Business rules engine:** The business rules engine externalizes the key business rules from the customer master application and allows a lot more flexibility for the business to define and modify the business rules. Key business rules that will be considered are:
  - Data validation business rules
  - Data de-duplication/merging of business rules
  - Data synchronization business rules

  Externalization of business rules will provide the needed flexibility and adaptability for business requirements.

- **Metadata:** Metadata captures the description of the data. For each target attribute, metadata contains how the source data are extracted, cleansed and aggregated to reach the target. Metadata also captures the key business rules applied on the data.

- **Data synchronization:** Once the customer register is updated based on data from product systems, the data may need to be distributed to different product systems having the same customer data. For example a customer request for change of mobile number recorded on his credit card account will have to flow to other applications containing that customer's record. For this, all the records captured in the customer master, are distributed to the product applications as per defined business rules.

Getting the 'single customer master' program right is a challenging task for banks. This program involves understanding the processing/

analytical needs of the bank, understanding the data models and key attributes of various processing applications; it requires a well-defined mechanism to address data quality issues and technology products to support the single customer master application. Banks will need to revisit this program whenever there is a merger or acquisition or whenever a new segment of service is launched by the bank.

CHAPTER 6

Accounts/Deposits

The accounts/deposits application holds the master record of all account balances and transactions. Let us take a look at the evolution of accounts/deposits automation for banks.

MANUAL

In this case, the branch of a bank maintains a physical file with account details and transaction details organized into various ledgers and folios. Customer transactions can only happen at the home branch. All the withdrawals will be done after manual verification of the signature and account balance. All the credits/debits will be entered manually into the register. A branch is open to customers only for a few hours and the staff need to reconcile the books manually in the remaining hours. This has significant disadvantages like poor customer service, high manpower, error-prone process and lack of scalability.

BRANCH AUTOMATION

The next level is branch automation where all the accounts and transactions in a branch are automated at the branch level application. These applications are hosted within the servers in the branch. While branch automation is a big leap forward, it still has the disadvantage of localization of data limiting the transactions to its own branch. Information is spread across multiple branch servers making it difficult for the management to get a comprehensive overview of operations. This approach also has other disadvantages such as having to distribute the application across all the branches every time there is a change and lacks in sophisticated business continuity. This solution is not capable of supporting branch channels located away from the bank, like ATMs, internet banking and mobile banking.

CORE BANKING

Core banking solutions refer to centralized banking functions like accounts/deposits to which all the debits/credits across the branches/channels, be it ATMs, online or debit card, will be posted. All the branches, ATMs, POS terminals will be connected to the bank's data centre through a secured wide area network. Core banking is a highly scalable transaction processing system capable of handling millions of transactions across multiple channels over the network. These systems are hosted in best-in-class data centres with all the necessary business continuity arrangements. Early implementations of core banking solutions were custom built legacy solutions, however in the last two decades or so, a significant number of modern off-the-shelf core banking solutions with high configurability and scalability have come up with hundreds of successful implementations across the world.

A centralized accounts/deposits application is at the heart of modern retail banking technology and hence we will deal with this in detail in the remaining part of the chapter. Let us look at some of the key architectural aspects of the core banking solution like:

* Service oriented architecture
* Real-time multi-channel capability

Service Oriented Architecture

Accounts/Deposits systems have been in existence for quite some time and one of the most popular implementations across banks has been using mainframe technology. This technology supports large volumes of back ground transactions as well as a large user base. Mainframe systems are secure, reliable and capable of processing a large number of transactions. They also support hundreds of user logins simultaneously by providing simple data entry or query screens, popularly referred to as "Green Screens". These systems do not offer rich GUI or context sensitive data population or a dynamic screen. Users need to capture the transaction or query data and submit their request for processing by the mainframe system. A mainframe system does not spend any processing time on the screens while the data entry is being made, which is a reason why these systems can handle such large user connections.

There are certain disadvantages to this architecture. The user interface provided by these screens was not intuitive and did not motivate bank staff to use these screens to service their customers. Most of the systems that bank staff, as well as customers, use in real life are intuitive, dynamic and context sensitive and hence their expectations and demands towards banking systems are also raised. Secondly, these screens were designed based on the application. For example there are different applications and different screens to query customer records, add customer records, query an account, query or create a deposit etc. For a single customer transaction, bank staff needed to navigate across the screens of different applications to be able to address the customer's needs. Finally, with the advent of new channels, the tight coupling between the channel and the processing results in duplication of functionalities specific to each processing.

Banks have adopted one of the following two options to modernize the core banking platform:

- One of the modernization options for banks is to use large, complex programs to replace the legacy core banking systems with modern, service oriented open systems that can interface and integrate with a multitude of channels. Most of these replacements are an implementation of a market product available from various vendors. This option comes with high costs and business risks. Due to the complex web of interfaces between different applications, core banking replacement needs to be planned in close consideration with other ongoing enhancements and business programs across the banks. Most of the modern banking platforms support open architecture and integration with various channels and back-office applications.

- Banks can modernize the legacy host application by re-architecting the landscape with the usage of service oriented architecture and middleware components. Service oriented architecture helps banks to interface and integrate with a wider variety of channels and applications while retaining their investments in the legacy systems. In service oriented architecture, core systems are exposed as services that can be invoked by other systems, like channels, using well-defined interfaces and protocols. Some examples of services are customer queries, balance checks, recent transactions, posting transactions, etc. Service oriented architecture clearly separates the systems that require service and systems that offer the service by a thick wall. Once service oriented architecture is made use of, systems providing the service can be replaced/modernized/upgraded without impacting all the systems using that service, as long as it is ensured that service definitions are not altered in the process. Similarly systems offering the service do not bother about the technology or implementation details of various applications invoking the service as long as the application is authorized and compliant to the service definition. This flexibility enables banks to modernize their systems in an incremental fashion.

In service oriented architecture, various transaction processing systems like ATM, POS, teller, use the services offered by the core banking system to query the balance, query the transactions and post the transactions. Similarly on the user interface side, aggregator applications are built that can avail of the services offered by various core product systems and show comprehensive customer data to branch, call centre and back-office users. Bank staff need not depend on so called 'green screens' for their operations but can use intuitive GUIs that have all the relevant data sourced from multiple applications using their exposed services. Service oriented architecture has helped banks as well as many other organizations to modernize the architecture and open it up a bit more while retaining the investments in legacy technology. This approach also helps banks to plan the modernization of the legacy technology in a phased manner without adverse impacts to their daily business.

Real-time Multi-channel Capability

Until recently, branches and ATM/POS devices were the only channels that the core banking systems needed to support. All the customers' transactions on their accounts either in the branch or at the ATM/POS need instantaneous authorization which can be provided only after updating the available balance with the transaction amount. This ensures that no two transactions can debit the same balance allowing a customer to withdraw more than what is available in the account. Similarly, other transactions like latest balance check and current day transactions will also need to access the core banking application for the latest information. Early core banking systems were designed to process the transactions generated from the branches and ATM/POS devices, as well as provide bank staff with various screens to query customer, account and balance information. Operating hours of the branches are limited thus leaving ATM/POS as the only channels requiring nearly 24x7 instant authorization. Another important aspect that has to be considered for 24x7 instant authorization is the IT processing time window for the bank.

Every organization IT system has a processing calendar that starts with "Beginning Of Day (BOD) processing", "day processing" and "End-Of-Day (EOD) processing". Usually real-time transactions are processed in the Day processing window, leaving the BOD and EOD windows for background processing tasks like interest computation, reports, system date change, house-keeping, etc. BOD and EOD processes are usually run outside the branch transaction timings and hence do not impact the branch transactions. But BOD and EOD processes may impact the 24x7 instant authorization required by ATM/POS channels, at least for a part of the window. To support transactions during the system maintenance window, typically "stand-in" processing is introduced in which balances from the core banking are copied to the stand-in processing server at the beginning of the system maintenance window. All the ATM/POS transactions will be authorized based on these balances which will be updated and transactions are authorized accordingly. Once the

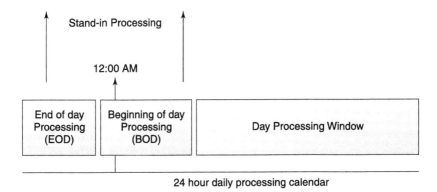

Fig. 6.1 *Typical Daily Processing Window*

"day processing" window starts, all the transactions from the "stand-in-processing" server will be posted to the core banking system to reflect the correct balances. Figure 6.1 presents a typical processing window on a banking business day.

However, with the advent of many new 24x7 channels like online banking, mobile banking and customer call centres, the number of users requiring transactions as well as transaction processing window requirements have increased significantly. In an ideal world, a core banking system should be able to process all the requests for balance checks, current day transactions and credit/debit transactions originating from different channels in real time and within the acceptable response times. Some of the modern core banking products are able to offer real-time transaction authorization and multi-channel integration with a single source of truth shown across the channels.

However many of the legacy systems may not be able to process all the requests for balance checks, balance update and current day transactions in real time. So these banks have designed work around solutions like batch posting of certain transactions, delayed reflection of balances and transactions across channels etc., to ensure support of multi-channels. Table 6.1 shows typical differences between "real-time" and "legacy" core banking solutions.

Table 6.1 Real-time vs. Legacy Core Banking Solutions

Feature	Real-time	Legacy
Balance enquiry	Latest balance is always available across channels	Some channels, like online banking etc., may show the balance as of the start of the day
Current day transactions	Visible across all channels	In some channels, current day transaction details can be seen only from the next day
Transaction posting	Always ensures that balances are updated correctly irrespective of the initiation channel and confirmation will be sent back to the customer immediately.	Always ensures that balances are updated correctly irrespective of the initiation channel and confirmation will be sent back to the customer immediately. However in some channels like online banking, beyond regular hours, transactions can be captured but posting may happen in batch. Confirmation will be sent to the customer only after posting is successful.

Table 6.2 Accounts/Deposits Applications-Snapshot

Actors	The product management team will use this application to define and configure the accounts/deposits products. Branch/Operations staff will use this application for opening accounts, and activation and servicing related activities. Customers will transact on their accounts through various channels like a branch, ATM, online banking etc.
Interfaces	Accounts/Deposits application will be integrated with all the channels, payments applications, customer master applications. This application will also interface with the finance application to feed all the transactions for financial accounting.
Key data	Account, deposit details, product configuration details, transaction details, debit cards and cheque book details are some of the key data maintained by this application.

Figure 6.2 presents the key functionalities within the centralized account/deposits platform.

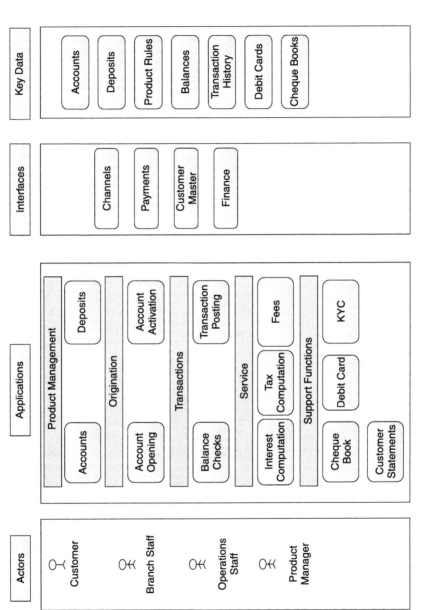

Fig. 6.2 *Accounts/Deposits Applications*

Applications components are described in the following sections.

Product Management

Banks continuously innovate to offer the most relevant products to customers to retain their customer base as well as attract new customers. To launch a new product, a bank should be able to define various attributes of the product in the core banking system, for example defining minimum balance requirements, charges, and withdrawal limits etc., for a new type of account. In legacy core banking applications, launching a new product may need the involvement of an IT team to capture the features of the new product or modifications to an existing product. The IT team may have to configure or alter the product rules hard coded into the applications. However, modern core banking applications offer product management capabilities to configure account/deposit products in order to be able to launch new products or modify/enhance existing products. Legacy applications will have little or no configuration facilities, whereas modern core banking solutions offer advanced product management capabilities. Banks offer various account/deposit products to their customers with different features according to the customer segment. Some examples of accounts are:

- Salary accounts
- Student accounts
- Senior citizen accounts
  Similarly some examples of term deposits are:
- Term deposit
- Flexi deposit
- Recurring deposit

Banks also introduce new products or modify the features of the existing products from time to time. The product management component allows the product management team to define and configure various business rules without the involvement of IT teams. For example, some of the business rules that can be configured for accounts are:

- Minimum monthly average balance
- Interest rate on the balance
- Number of cheques provided
- Number of ATM withdrawals

Some of the business rules that can be configured for deposits are:

- Deposit interest rate
- Minimum allowed deposit
- Maximum allowed deposit
- Premature withdrawal allowed

Once the new product is created it will be deployed on to the accounts/deposits module so that the product can be launched.

Origination

Origination is the process of capturing the customer application, supporting documentation and performing the necessary validations and activating the account.

Opening an account: Opening an account is the process of creating a new account for an existing customer/new customer. This process is usually handled at the branch or by the back office where all the customer applications are processed. Some banks offer their customers the basic option of opening an account directly through their website, using which customers fill in the details and submit the application. Banks also offer the facility of opening an account to their existing customers through internet banking.

It is mandatory for banks to follow KYC norms. According to these, they need to capture, verify and maintain a customer's identification and proof of residence before activating an account. The account opening process checks the existence of the customer record in the master and associates it with the account. If a customer record does not exist, a request for the creation of a new customer will be initiated. However, if the customer record already exists along with KYC compliance, then the account may be activated automatically.

Transactions

Customers operate their accounts using various channels like a branch, ATM, online banking etc. In essence, accounts/deposits products should enable successful and correct processing of these transactions. The level of coupling with channel applications as well as the nature of coupling (real-time/batch) varies with different implementations. Advanced core banking platforms offer well defined services for low coupling and real time transaction processing whereas legacy platforms may have tight coupling and batch processing. Highly scalable real time transaction processing that offers multi-channel capability is a key differentiator for a modern bank.

Key functions that need to be supported by an accounts/deposits application are:

* **Check balance:** This service provides the latest balance in the account in response to customer/staff queries. This service may be used in multiple scenarios, e.g., a customer querying the balance through an ATM or the latest balance being updated on teller or call centre application screens.

* **Recent transactions:** This service provides the most recent transactions posted on to the account including current day transactions. It may be used in scenarios like customer queries at an ATM machine, or through online banking.

* **Posting:** This service enables various applications to post the debit/credit bookings on to customer accounts and receive confirmation. This service may be used in multiple scenarios like a customer withdrawing money at an ATM or bill payment through online banking.

Service

All the accounts/deposits need to be serviced for interest, tax and customer fees.

* **Interest computation:** This is a batch process that is run on a periodic basis to compute the interest amount. Interest computation is based on the account type, account configuration, applicable interest rates and account balances maintained. Typically, the interest computation process will use end-of-day balance history

to arrive at the interest component. Once computed, interest amounts will be accrued and posted to the accounts at predefined intervals to reflect the balances as per the interest calendar.

- **Tax computation:**   Banks may have to deduct tax on interest and other proceeds as per the applicable tax regime. The tax amount will be deducted from the interest and will be credited to the accounts of the tax authorities. A tax report will be generated to the customer to enable him/her to reclaim the amount.

- **Fees and charges:**   Each account/deposit may have different fees and charges based on product definition and configuration. Some examples of fees and charges are monthly account fees, charges for not maintaining the minimum balance, number of ATM transactions, number of cash withdrawals etc. This application will process all the transaction data from the accounts/deposits system based on the rules to arrive at the fee amount. Once computed, fees and charges will be posted to the customer's account.

Support Functions

Accounts/Deposits will also have the following additional features:

- **Cheque book management:**   This application component maintains the cheque inventory of each account and supports the processes of ordering and re-ordering cheque books.

- **Debit card management:**   This application component maintains the debit cards associated with a particular account/deposit. This application will maintain the card details, activation/de-activation and re-issue of the cards.

- **KYC:**   This application component manages the workflow and documentation related to KYC compliance for its customers. This application will also maintain the KYC documentation electronically for future compliance.

- **Customer statements:**   This application produces the customers' statements including all the transactions on their accounts on a monthly, quarterly or semi-annual basis. Statements will be generated either in electronic form or in physical (on paper) form and formatting will be aligned with the branded stationery of the bank. All the statements in the paper form will be printed in the mailing room for dispatch to customers.

CHAPTER 7

Lending

Retail lending comprises all the products under which a bank lends money to its retail customers. Retail lending offers a stable diversified asset portfolio for the banks. Retail lending products can be broadly categorized under the heads of secured and unsecured lending. Secured lending refers to lending products like mortgages or auto loans where the underlying asset is used as collateral against the loan. Unsecured lending refers to products like credit cards, personal loans and student loans which are disbursed without any underlying security. A bank's profitability on retail lending products is sensitive to volumes and credit quality, and banks will need both scale and quality to be able to achieve a profitable retail lending portfolio.

The key steps of a lending life cycle are depicted in Figure 7.1.

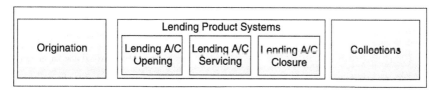

Fig. 7.1 *Lending Life Cycle*

Key systems in a lending process can be classified as origination, product systems and collections.

- **Origination:** This application manages the processes between a customer submitting an application and the bank's decision to approve/reject the loan. This application automates the various checks, approvals and verification to be carried out to arrive at the decision. Banks may have a common configurable origination system across lending products.
- **Product systems:** This application manages the opening of the loan account in the system, loan account servicing and loan account closure. System requirements vary from product to

product and banks will have different systems for different lending products. Also, there are a number of commercially available off-the-shelf systems covering various lending products.

- **Collections:** This application manages the collections life cycle for non-performing assets of a bank. Banks may have a common configurable collections system across lending products.

These applications are further explained below.

ORIGINATION

This is the process that happens between the customers submitting the loan application and the bank's decision on that application. A loan application will move through several stages within the bank as given below:

- Customer background check
- Credit history check
- Loan eligibility check
- Valuation (in case of mortgage)
- Legal
- Credit
- Documentation check

Loan application turn-around time is one of the crucial differentiators for a bank and the origination process has to be efficient and fast. Banks also need to ensure that the application does not get held up in the hand-off process between departments. One of the key technology enablers for achieving an efficient process for origination is Business Process Management (BPM). In BPM parlance, each business transaction like a customer loan application is referred to as a 'case'. BPM technology enables the following features needed for the origination process:

- Handling of a large volume of loan requests/cases efficiently and in a timely manner.
- Enabling a business to define the process steps and sequence for processing each loan request.
- Ensuring that all the process steps are carried out in the right sequence and that no process step is missed out.

- Ensuring that no case is missed out in the hand-off process between different departments.
- Providing the management with an overview of the loan application process.

Typically a business transaction receives an input from a customer, processes it through various steps both manual and automatic, usually by different departments within the organization to produce the outcome expected by customer. A business process can spread across multiple systems and departments and BPM helps tailor these individual services together to automate that business process. The business process management is about orchestrating the services of various applications as well as manual interventions to complete a business transaction. A bank may have different IT systems catering to the needs of different departments like credit, legal, finance etc., but a business process like origination cuts across these IT systems and BPM plays a key role in bringing the relevant services from these applications together in a flexible manner.

There are number of software products and solutions available for implementation of a BPM solution. Building blocks for a BPM solution are mentioned in Figure 7.2 and are further explained below.

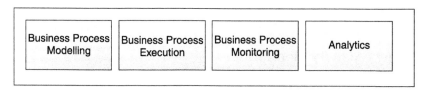

| Business Process Modelling | Business Process Execution | Business Process Monitoring | Analytics |

Fig. 7.2 *Business Process Management*

Business Process Modelling

The functionality of this component is to model the process in terms of inputs, events, decision points and the sequence of process steps etc., needed to complete a business process. Process steps can be automated or manual. For example in a typical origination process, there are a number of process steps which will be carried out in a particular sequence as given below:

- KYC check
- Credit check
- Valuation (in case of mortgages)
- Legal
- Documentation verification

Within a bank some of these steps like KYC check, document verification may be done manually whereas others are automated. A business process is modelled by capturing both manual and automated process steps in the right sequence with the appropriate dependencies between them captured.

Business Process Execution

This is the run-time environment for executing the business model developed as part of the previous exercise. Each case navigates through various manual and automated processes and the decision flow as per definition, to provide the required outcome. For example the incoming application record will be routed to the sub-process for a KYC check and if the outcome is positive, then it will be routed to the credit check process step etc. Some of the process steps, such as verification of documents may be manual, which means the user will have to manually verify the documentation and mark the case as verified.

Business Activity Monitoring

It is important for banks to ensure that all new applications are processed in line with the service levels and no opportunities are lost or missed out. Business activity monitoring helps to monitor all the open cases in the system, their current status and especially the cases which are pending at a process step beyond the agreed service levels. Necessary escalations will be done automatically to the supervisors, as per the configuration in the business activity monitoring system.

Analytics

This component provides the analytical information about the cases that are handled by the system, for example, the number of applications received, number of applications rejected because of credit check, number of applications accepted, total value of applications in process etc. This will help the management to monitor the business process performance and take necessary actions.

Another component of the origination process is the automated decision engine.

Automated Decision Engine

This application interfaces with various components like KYC check, credit scoring, loan eligibility etc., and helps in making the final lending decision. Decision engines are typically rule based systems and consider several parameters to arrive at the decision. These rules can be configured/modified by users as per credit policy. The automated decision engine enables innovative origination practices like instant approval of loans etc.

LENDING PRODUCT SYSTEMS

Lending product systems maintain the lending accounts and support the various business transactions on the lending account until the loan closure. In the following sections, we will discuss the product systems for credit cards, mortgages and auto loans.

Credit cards

The credit card product is a combination of "payment" and "unsecured lending" products. A credit card is one of the most widely used cashless payment mechanisms across the world. Using a credit card is a simple procedure for customers and the payment process is usually completed in a few seconds after swiping the card at the Point-Of-Sale (POS) device. However, underlying these transactions there are several industry players, complex networks and processing systems to enable the transaction. Before getting into the credit card processing systems, let us take a quick look at the players involved and the high level transaction flow for credit card payments. Apart from the customer and the merchant, there are three major industry players in a card payment transaction namely, the issuing bank, acquiring bank and card scheme.

Issuing bank

The issuing bank offers credit cards to its customers; these may be issued to existing customers or on a stand-alone basis. The issuing bank's responsibility includes a credit check of the customer, maintaining the card account, invoicing and collections. Issuing banks have to become members of a card scheme like VISA, MasterCard etc., to be able to issue the cards of that scheme. Banks in the issuer role deal mainly with retail customers.

Acquiring bank

Acquiring banks offer point-of-sale devices to merchants so that they can accept card payments from their customers. Point-of-sale devices are connected to an acquiring bank server. The responsibilities of the acquiring bank include merchant accounts, POS connectivity, routing of transactions for authorization and merchant settlement. Banks in the acquirer role mainly deal with merchants. Apart from POS, banks may also provide online payment gateways to enable merchants to support online payments for e-commerce transactions. Banks also accept credit cards on their ATMs for cash transactions but will only be able accept the cards from the schemes that the bank is a member of.

Card scheme

Card schemes like VISA and MasterCard provide secure global networks connecting acquiring banks and issuing banks across the globe, providing unmatched convenience to customers. Card schemes are responsible for managing the network, promoting the brand, settlement between acquirers/issuers and dispute resolution. An acquirer bank can be assured of the money from the issuing bank for purchases on its POS devices, even though there is no direct relationship with the customer swiping the card, as this is assured by the card scheme.

Figure 7.3 presents the key players in a card scheme and the interaction between them.

The key transaction steps are described below:

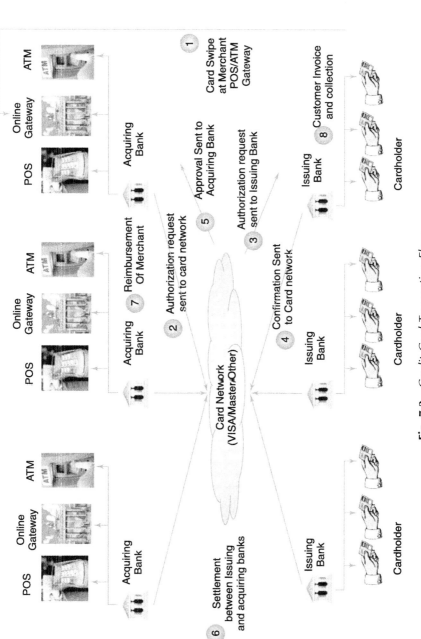

Fig. 7.3 *Credit Card Transaction Flow*

Step 1   Customers use the card issued by their bank to perform one of the following activities:

- Swipe the card at a merchant POS for purchases made/services utilized
- Withdrawal of cash at an ATM
- Use the card to pay for online purchases through a payment gateway

Step 2   The transaction is routed to an acquiring bank server by the POS device/ATM/gateway and reaches the high performance 'switch' for appropriate routing. All the card transactions of other issuing banks are routed to the card scheme network for authorization. Transactions of the cards issued by the acquirer ("On Us transactions") are routed to internal systems for processing.

Step 3   The card scheme validates the card and further routes the transaction to the issuing bank for authorization of the transaction.

Step 4   After authentication, the issuing bank validates the transaction amount against the customer's remaining credit limit and authorizes the card scheme network about the transaction.

Step 5   The card scheme informs the acceptance (or rejection) of the transaction to the acquiring bank which in turn will pass it on to the POS/ATM/gateway to complete the customer transaction.

Step 6   The card scheme will perform the settlement between acquiring banks and issuer banks on a net basis. Issuing banks will pay for all the transactions made by its customers across merchant locations and across acquiring banks. The card scheme will reimburse this money across acquirers whose POS devices/online gateways/ ATMs have been used for transactions. The card scheme will charge issuers and acquirers for the network, settlement and other services provided.

Step 7   The acquiring bank will reimburse the merchant for all the purchases made at that merchant POS. Acquiring banks will charge a commission on the amount paid to the merchants.

Step 8   The issuing bank will send an invoice to its customers for all the card purchases as per the billing cycle. The issuing bank is responsible for collections and holds the credit risk against potential default of the card holder. Credit offered using credit cards does not have any collateral and is unsecured. Usually card holders get up to 45 days of free credit before they pay the issuer bank. Issuing banks will make money from annual card charges and interest rates charged on outstanding amounts beyond the due date. For issuing banks, it is a fine balance between risk and interest revenue. The longer the payments are due, the higher the interest income and also the higher the risk of default.

Above we have given a description of a high level transaction; there are several variations and several alternate scenarios (transaction slips, additional authorization for online transactions, refunds, disputes) that are possible in card processing.

From the card transaction life cycle to the technology and systems for processing cards, credit cards technology is one of the most commoditized solutions and various solution options are available in the market. One of the key drivers for the standardization of credit card solutions is the business model; here interfaces and communication standards are defined by the two large card schemes providing high standardization and interoperability. Such standardization of services and features enables a number of solution options for banks implementing cards technology.

Some of the solution options are mentioned below:

- **Credit card solution products:** A card processing system can be implemented using off-the-shelf card processing solutions. This solution is hosted in the bank's data centre and operated by the bank's staff.

- **Hosted cards platform:** A hosted solution comes with the card product installed and managed in its data centre by a third party provider. Banks need to build their card operations around the hosted solution and they need not have any software or hardware installation for card operations.

- **Fully outsourced:** Also called 'white labelling', in this approach a third party provider offers card solutions, necessary infrastructure, data centre and also business operations. Cards will be branded under the issuing bank's name and overall customer relationship and credit risk are managed by the issuing bank leaving the rest of the functions to the third party.

In the rest of the chapter we will mainly focus on the issuing bank's solution as it is related to retail banking. Figure 7.4 represents an overview of an issuing bank's cards processing application.

Table 7.1 Credit Card Applications-Snapshot

Actors	Banks' operations staff will use this application to issue credit cards, dispatch PIN details, send card statements and receive payments.
	Customer card transactions at an ATM/POS and online gateways will be routed to this application for authorization.
Interfaces	Credit card application interfaces with all the channels including branch, call centre, online and mobile banking for providing access to bank staff as well as customers.
	This application interfaces with finance and data warehouse applications to share the transactions data for accounting, analytics and management information.
	This application also interfaces with the payments application to process receipts and interfaces with the collections application to manage overdue payments.
Key data	Key data elements maintained by this application are card account information, transaction history, plastic card details, PIN details and analytical information.

The application components of an issuer's card solution are described below.

Account management

- **Card account management:** This application allows the bank operations team to open the card account with the necessary customer details. Bank staff will also set the necessary limits on the card account as derived in the origination process.
- **Plastic cards:** This application manages the plastic card inventory and association of plastic cards to the credit card account. It will enable personalization of cards, including embossing and security measures. This application also processes lost/stolen card requests as well as re-issue of cards.

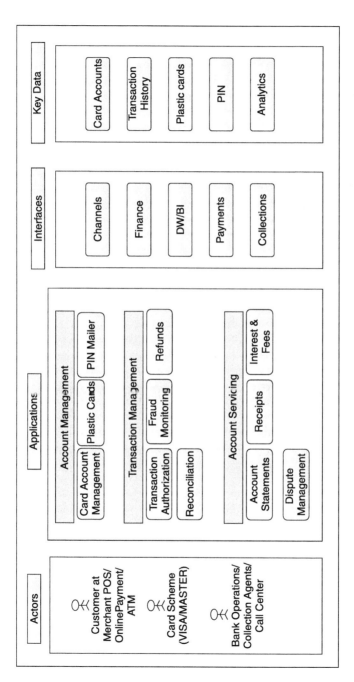

Fig. 7.4 *Card Issuer Applications*

- **PIN mailer:** This application enables secure printing and dispatch of the PIN mailer for a customer's credit card.

Transaction management

Key transaction features of the card applications are validating the authorization requests received over the card scheme network, processing the debit, credit transactions and invoicing/statements.

- **Transaction authorization:** This component validates the requests received from card schemes for the card transactions of its customers. This is a high performance component that should be available 24x7 and provide faster response times.

- **Fraud monitoring:** This component monitors the card transactions for identifying potential fraudulent activities. Fraud monitoring uses underlying customer behavioural analytics to identify unusual patterns. Fraud monitoring alerts will be tracked to closure to reduce/eliminate fraud.

- **Refunds:** This component processes the customer returns and merchant refunds to credit the money back into the card account.

- **Reconciliation:** The card scheme performs the settlement between the issuing bank and acquiring bank based on the transactions of the issuing bank's customers on the acquiring bank's POS/ATM or online gateway channels. This component performs the reconciliation of authorized transactions with the card scheme settlement.

Account servicing

- **Account statements:** This component produces the account statements for customers depending on the billing cycle. Some banks offer a flexible billing cycle to their customers. This component interfaces with printing devices for printing on branded stationery and also generates electronic statements to be distributed via e-mail.

- **Receipts:** This component handles the customer's payments against the credit card bills. The customer's payments will be credited into the account and balances will be adjusted accordingly.

- **Interest & fees:** This component handles the computation of interest on the outstanding balances as per the card features. It also computes various fees like cash fees, annual fee, add-on-card fees etc. Interest and fees will be charged to the card account and will be part of the next account statement.

- **Dispute management:** This component enables the banks to manage any disputes arising from the customers on the transaction entries in the account statement. This is a case management application with configurable workflows to automatically route and track customer disputes. These disputes need to be taken up with the card scheme and acquiring banks for resolution, if necessary.

Mortgages

Mortgages are typically the most secured loans for banks (at least they were until 2008!) as they are disbursed against the property as collateral, provided the credit history and credit eligibility of the customer are thoroughly verified. It is evident from the recent sub-prime crisis that even mortgage loans can result in significant losses if the customer's ability and willingness to repay the loan are not validated enough. This crisis also re-emphasized the basic lending principle that repayment ability of the borrower and purpose of the loan are far more important than the collateral for the loan, as collateral value may erode significantly in the times of crisis.

As described above, mortgage lending processing systems cater to the three broad functionalities of origination, mortgage processing and collections. Mortgage origination is about receiving the application forms, conducting a legal review of project documentation, assessing the project viability, valuation, and finally verifying the customer's credit history and loan eligibility. Mortgage origination has to deal with significant documentation, interact with a number of players and complete a larger number of steps as compared to other lending products. From a technology perspective there are two key enablers for the efficiency and productivity of the mortgage origination process.

- **Document management system:** During the origination process it is necessary to handle a large number of documents to perform the various checks. The document management system enables automation and will eliminate the need for transporting physical documents between various departments. It links all the loan documentation to the loan application number and makes it available electronically to various stakeholders like legal experts, valuation specialists, bank staff etc. Paper documents continue to be very important, however electronic versions of these documents stored and linked in a document management system will assist the bank in many ways. It will be possible for the various departments to retrieve the documents pertaining to any loan almost instantly and simultaneously. Documents stored can be archived for a longer duration for any future requirement or investigation.

- **Workflow:** During the lifecycle of a mortgage origination process, there are number of stakeholders who will need to perform certain key actions on the application. These actions/approvals are typically from people who are specialized in different areas like valuation experts, legal experts, credit managers etc. Workflow applications keep track of the life cycle and sequence of the steps and will present the application in the queue of an appropriate specialist. This will enable the specialists to focus on clearing their workflows without worrying about the overall lifecycle.

Once the loan is approved, the customer will be intimated and the loan account will be opened in the mortgage processing system for further processing.

Figure 7.5 presents the key application modules within the mortgage processing system.

Components of a mortgage processing system are described in Table 7.2.

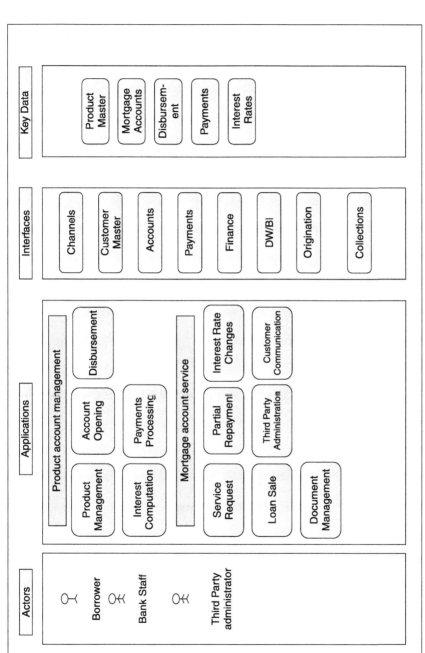

Fig. 7.5 *Mortgage Applications*

Table 7.2 Mortgage Applications-Snapshot

Actors	This system will be used by the bank's staff for opening an account and servicing the account. The customer will be able to get the necessary information on his/her mortgage account through customer channels. Banks may off-load some of the mortgage processing activities to third-parties, who in turn will access the system.
Interfaces	The mortgage processing system interfaces with both indirect channels used by staff and customer channels used by customers to provide the relevant information. This system interfaces with the customer master application to uniquely identify the mortgage customers across all the products utilized. This system interfaces with accounts, payments applications for receiving mortgage payments from customers. This system sends the mortgage transaction data to finance systems for accounting purposes. This system sends the mortgage data to the Data Warehouse (DW)/Business Intelligence (BI) application for management reporting and analytics. This system interfaces with the collections system to send the necessary data on overdue payments to initiate the collections process.
Key data	Product master data will contain details about the various mortgage products offered by the bank and the key attributes. Mortgage accounts data will contain all the details about the mortgage accounts, their balances and transaction details. This system will maintain disbursement needs and actual disbursement data. This system will also maintain all the customer payments due and actual payments information.

The application components of the mortgage processing system are described below:

Mortgage account management

- **Product management:** Each bank offers a set of mortgage products with varying features. Some of the characteristics of these loan products are fixed interest/variable interest rate, pre-payment penalty, loan tenure etc. Some of the special products are:

- **Teaser loans:** Offer discounted rates for the initial few years and then interest rates will be adjusted to market rates.

- **Hybrid:** This kind of mortgage offers a combination of fixed and variable rate of interest rates in a single loan. A part of the loan could be on a fixed rate and the remaining part on a variable rate. Alternatively, the initial few years can be at a fixed rate and later this becomes a variable rate loan.

- **Interest only:** In some countries, interest only loans require borrowers to pay interest at a minimum rate, giving the borrower the flexibility to pay the principal. At the end of the loan tenure, the borrower will have the option to pay the remaining principal and claim the ownership.

- **Offset accounts:** These loan accounts offer liquidity as well as the flexibility of low interest rates. In this product, along with the loan account, a banking account will be opened in the customer's name. Available balance in the banking account will be offset against the outstanding loan balance to compute the interest.

The product management component enables product owners to create mortgage products by configuring processing rules. Legacy mortgage processing systems will have product rules embedded inside the IT systems and will typically require an IT project to introduce a new product or modify the features of an existing product. However, the product management feature externalizes the business rules of the product and enables the business users to define a new product or modify the processing rules of an existing product.

- **Opening an account:** Once the origination process is completed, an account will be opened in the mortgage processing application with the customer's details, approved loan amount, agreed contractual terms like interest rates, disbursement and payment schedules. Access to the mortgage account is provided to customers through self-service channels like online banking for easy tracking.

- **Disbursement:** An estimated loan disbursement plan is captured as a part of opening the account. Loan disbursement can be in one tranche or several tranches depending on the nature of the property. The disbursement module enables bank staff to process disbursement requests as per the plan, validate the pre-conditions and process the payments.

- **Interest computation:** This process computes interest on outstanding loan amounts as per the loan account configuration. This is typically a monthly process running in batch mode. The interest computation process should also consider any balances in linked savings accounts, in case of offset loan products.

- **Payments processing:** This component captures and processes all the payments received on the loan accounts. Cheques, electronic transfer of funds, direct debit are some of the payment modes for loan instalments. This component will perform the necessary credit bookings into the loan account.

Mortgage account service

- **Service requests:** This component helps to process the customer's service requests during the life of the mortgage. Some of the mortgage related service requests are:
  - Change of address/contact details
  - Disbursement requests
  - Requests for documents like tax statements
  - Queries

These service requests are typically captured in the Customer Relationship Management (CRM) application and the operations team will take action on these requests in the mortgage processing application.

- **Partial repayment:** This component allows partial payment of the loan amount by borrowers. This component will process the customer's payments and update the loan account accordingly.

- **Change in interest rates:** This component allows mortgage product owners to capture the change of interest rate applicable across the portfolio at a specified effective date. This will also generate letters to the customers with details of the change. The new interest rate will be used by the interest computation process from the effective date onwards.

- **Loan sale:** This component will allow banks to sell the loan/ portfolio of loans to another bank/financing entity. This helps banks to reduce the assets in the balance sheet while still preserving the opportunity to retain the administration of the loan to earn a commission.

- **Third party administration:** Banks may choose to leverage services of a third party administration for processing the mortgage. In this case, administration is handled by another party for a commission. Loan account processing will receive the payments from third party administrators and the books will be updated accordingly.

- **Customer communication:** There are a number of letters that need to be generated to customers like information on loan sanctions, intimation of disbursement, change in interest rate, notices, etc. Mortgage processing will produce the necessary letters to be printed and dispatched to the customers.

- **Document management:** As discussed, document management is an enabler for efficient handling of a large number of documents in mortgage processing. This system will enable the loan account number to be linked with all the document images related to that loan. This enables bank staff to easily retrieve the relevant documents pertaining to a loan from any location.

The third group of applications related to mortgage processing are for collections and receivables. This group of applications caters to the bank's requirements for handling the delays in payments and defaults. These applications cater to the collections department within the bank to help them to effectively recover dues from borrowers. They also cater to the various stages of collections like pre-delinquency, delinquency and write-off. Default processing functionality also covers the needs related to selling the collateral and using the proceeds towards closure. One of the key features of the collections processing application is to arrive at an optimum collection strategy (e-mails, calls, letters etc.,) to increase the efficiency of collections. The collections module is described in detail later in this chapter.

Auto Finance

Auto finance applications cater to the bank's needs in supporting retail lending for auto finance. Workflow in the auto finance origination process is less complex compared to mortgage processing. Typically the documentation requirements, legal and valuation parameters and duration of auto loans are simpler compared to mortgage loans. The key functions pertaining to the auto loan core processing system are:

- **Opening an account:** A loan account is opened once the origination process is completed and the loan is approved.
- **Computation of interest:** Interest is computed on a monthly basis on the outstanding amount and posted to the loan account. The interest computation process here is a lot simpler than in mortgage processing, with fewer variations for processing.
- **Payments processing:** A customer's monthly payments will be processed and credited to the loan account.

For all the loan accounts that fall under the collection life cycle, data will be sent to the collections system for recovery process.

COLLECTIONS

The collections process deals with handling out-of-order loan accounts where payments are due but not received for more than a certain number of days. Typically, central banks set the guidelines for treating non-performing assets, for example, all loan accounts where the due date for repayment of a loan instalment has exceeded more than 90 days, should be considered as a Non-Performing Asset (NPA). Banks will not be able to recognize any further revenue from these accounts until repayments are made and the loan account returns to performing status. The collection process is about following up with non performing accounts for collecting the dues effectively. The efficiency of the process is very important as collections directly add to the bottom-line and banks need to deploy limited resources on those accounts where the chances of recovery are higher. When a particular loan account is non-performing for more than a certain number of days, it will have to be written-off and recovery procedures need to be initiated. Recovery procedures include sale of collateral if available or debt sale to a third party or even a complete write-off.

The collections process is effort intensive and it is important to have an automated workflow based system to handle the collections process. It is also important to deploy the right collection strategy depending on the life cycle of the account, customer behavioural analytics and earlier interactions to improve the efficiency of the collections process. The collections system will process all the non-performing loan accounts from various lending product systems to arrive at the optimal collection strategy (mail, phone call etc.). Collection agents will implement the collection strategy and capture the results of the interactions in the system. Loan accounts where satisfactory payments are received will go out of the collections workflow.

Figure 7.6 represents the key applications of the collections processing system

Table 7.3 Collections Applications-Snapshot

Actors	Collection agents use this application to efficiently follow up with the customers for overdue payments. This system also generates letters, e-mails to borrowers as per collection strategy.
Interfaces	All the lending applications like credit cards, mortgage, auto and personal loan management systems will feed data of all non performing accounts. Payments/Accounts systems will feed all the payments received on accounts in the collection life-cycle. This system sends the summarized information to data warehouse/BI solution for reporting on the collections process. This system also interfaces with various rating agencies on borrower credit scoring data.
Key data	The collection system will maintain: A list of non performing accounts Collection strategy arrived at for follow-up Customer contact history for collections

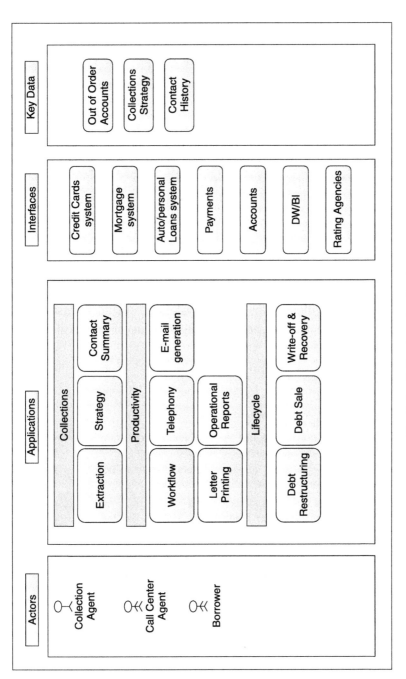

Fig. 7.6 *Collections Applications*

The application components for collection are described below.

Collections

- **Extraction:** This process will pick up all the loan accounts where the date of repayment of the instalment has been crossed but payment has not been received as per the defined criteria. These accounts will be loaded into the collection system for further processing.

- **Strategy:** This application will process various parameters like customer transaction history, credit scoring, overall relationship with the bank, previous contact history etc., to arrive at the optimal collections strategy to contact the customer for recovery.

- **Contact summary:** A summary of all the contacts with customers for collection is recorded for future processing and reference. This component will capture the responses to all forms of interactions like telephone calls, e-mails or printed letters.

Productivity

- **Workflow:** As there are a number of collections records to be processed by collection agents, bank officials, legal teams etc., the collection system will typically present the workflow for the agents to show the list of accounts that need follow-up. The workflow system will help to track each collection case for closure effectively.

- **Telephony:** Loan accounts that have been identified as being eligible for phone based follow-up are shown on the collection agents' screens. The telephony interface enables them to dial the customer after inspecting the case. This will help save time in connecting with the customer.

- **E-mail:** Loan accounts identified for e-mail based follow-up will be sent to this module along with the full details of the account and the amount due. This application will automatically generate e-mails to all the borrowers as per the standard templates defined.

- **Printing letters:** This component will generate letters for the collection accounts identified for letter based follow-up. Letters will be generated in the defined template, including customer loan and repayment details.

Lifecycle

These applications support debt restructuring, write-off and recovery processes.

- **Debt restructuring:** It is important for the banks to support the customers in temporary distress and help them to repay the loan. This will not only help banks recover dues but also gain customer loyalty. This component helps to capture any restructuring terms like reduction of interest rate, reduction of interest or principal amount, payment holiday etc. This information will also be sent back to product applications to update the account information.

- **Debt sale:** Banks may sell off the bad debts to a third party and this component helps to capture the debt sale information in the collection system. This information will also be sent back to the product systems to close the loan accounts and feed finance applications appropriately.

- **Write-off & recovery:** This component will be used to issue the loan recall notice and also write-off the loan proceeds in the system. This function also sends the data back to the loan system to update the data accordingly. This process involves collateral recovery in case of a write-off. Functionalities include workflow for legal documentation, valuation, auction etc. The recovery process is mainly applicable to secured loans like home loans or auto loans.

CHAPTER 8
Payments

An efficient payment system is the backbone of any country's economy. Fast and cost-efficient transfer of funds is a key characteristic of a good banking system. One of the key services offered by banks, apart from safe keeping of money, is to provide multiple payment options according to the customers' needs. One of the oldest and still popular methods for payments is by cash. But cash payments need the physical presence of the customer at the time of the transaction which can be inconvenient and is unnecessary in most cases. For example to pay the rent or a telephone bill by cash, the customer first needs to go to a branch or ATM to withdraw cash and then go to the payee or his agent to complete the transaction. Cash transactions are also expensive from the bank's perspective due to the costs involved in physical handling of cash and branch footfalls for cash withdrawals. Finally, cash transactions do not leave a trace and many governments have put restrictions on the value of cash transactions. Electronic cash transactions are most convenient and cost-efficient compared to cash transactions both from customers' and banks' perspective. Payments by retail customers are usually small in value, high in volume and predominantly within the country. In a payment transaction, the payee and payer may have accounts with different banks and hence the need for movement of funds across the banks to complete such transactions. The interbank clearing function facilitates such movement of funds across banks to successfully complete payment transactions. The interbank clearing function is provided by different players like commercial organizations, central bank institutions or industry bodies depending on the electronic payment mechanism.

Table 8.1 shows key payment options for low-value and domestic payments that are relevant from a retail banking perspective.

Table 8.1 Retail Payment Services

Payment Option	Payment Scenarios	Interbank Clearing
Cheque payments	Customer to customer Customer to business Business to customer	Cheque clearing system
Card payments (ATM, POS and Electronic Gateways)	Customer to business	Card scheme (Visa/ MasterCard)
Electronic funds transfer	Customer to customer Customer to business Business to customer	National electronic funds transfer clearing system
Direct entry – Debits Direct entry – Credits	Business to customer	Direct entry clearing system
Bill payments	Customer to business	National bill payment system or Billing arrangements with banks
Mobile payments	Customer to customer Customer to business	National electronic funds transfer clearing system/service provider

These payment mechanisms are explained in the sections below.

CHEQUE PAYMENTS

One of the oldest mechanisms, still in use for manual payments is cheque payments. It is still popular but its usage is coming down rapidly. Cheques are paper based and manual effort intensive and hence it is the most expensive option (next only to cash) for banks to service payment requests. Initiatives have been taken by central banks and regulated associations to drive the payments to more efficient modes like POS, direct entry, electronic transfer of funds, etc. Measures are also being taken to improve the efficiency of processing cheques, such as electronically transmitting the image of the cheque from the bank processing centre to a regional/ national clearing system instead of sending a physical copy. Further advancements in ATM technology have enabled banks to offer real-time cheque deposit facilities using the cheque scanning feature with instant balance update and post clearance credits. This significantly reduces the manual effort involved in the processing in addition to increased availability and convenience to customers. With increased usage of smart-phone based mobile banking, banks have started offering mobile based cheque deposit facilities. Using these facilities, customers can use their mobile banking application to scan the cheque and submit it for processing without the need to visit a branch or an ATM.

Banks should be able to process the cheques drawn on other banks and deposited by a customer into his/her account, as well as cheques issued by its own customers but deposited in another bank account. Figure 8.1 explains the key scenarios in processing cheques.

Scenario A: A customer deposits the cheque drawn on the same bank. The bank will validate the cheque, validate the payer's signature, check/debit the balance in the payer's account and credit the payee.

Scenario B: A customer deposits the cheque drawn on another bank. The bank will route the cheque to a national/regional clearing system for processing and confirmation. Upon receipt of the confirmation, the customer's account will be credited. The clearing system will debit the payer's bank and credit the payee's bank on a net basis.

Scenario C: The clearing system forwards a cheque issued by a bank's customer, which is deposited in another bank. The bank will validate the cheque, validate the payer's signature, check/debit the balance and provide confirmation to the national clearing system, which will debit the payer's bank and credit the payee's bank on a net basis.

CARD PAYMENTS

A customer can use credit/debit cards to withdraw money from an ATM, pay merchants either through the POS device or using the online gateway. Some terms related to card payments are explained below.

Acquiring Service

Banks offer this service to merchant establishments to process their customers' payments. Point-of-sale (POS) devices are installed at

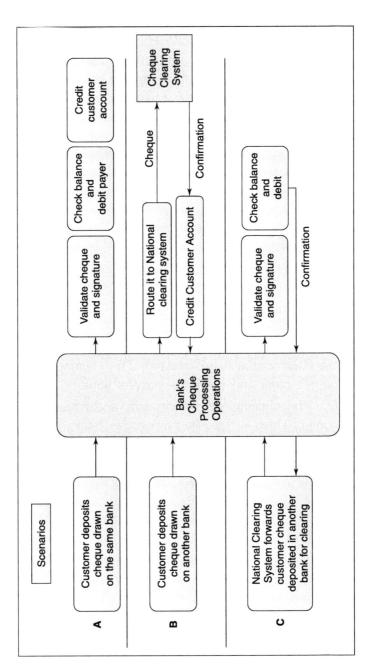

Fig. 8.1 *Cheque Processing Scenarios*

merchant establishments to process card payments by customers. Banks will need to take acquiring membership with various card schemes like Visa, MasterCard so that their POS devices can accept all the cards issued on those card schemes and process those payments. These POS devices are connected to the acquiring bank's data centre and to a high performance application called "switch". The switch application will validate the payment requests from various POS devices and route them to internal systems or to the appropriate card scheme for further routing to the issuing bank for authorization. This authorization information will be routed back to the POS device in real time so that the transaction can be completed at the merchant location.

Online Payment Gateways

Banks also offer payment gateway service for various e-commerce merchants to accept card payments. The payment gateway component is a software service which can be integrated into the e-commerce site. At the time of checkout, the e-commerce site will invoke the payment gateway function which is basically a software version of the POS device. The payment gateway application will be able to accept cards issued on card schemes subscribed to by the bank. A customer will enter the card details which will be routed to the 'switch' application for routing internally or over the card scheme network for authorization.

ATM/POS devices set up by the banks are not limited to cards issued by the bank. These devices usually accept a wide range of cards issued under various card schemes. Let us take a look at the following three possible payment scenarios with ATM/POS/online gateways.

Scenario 1: Bank A's customer transacting at bank A's ATM/POS/ online gateway: The transaction is routed to bank A's ATM/POS switch where it is verified that the card is issued by the bank itself and is routed to internal systems for further validation and authorization depending on the card type.

- For ATM/POS transactions, the request is forwarded to the "ATM/ POS authorization server" for validation and authorization. Upon confirmation, the transaction is posted to the accounts/deposits application.

- For credit card transactions, the request is forwarded to the credit card transaction processor for validation and authorization. Upon confirmation, the transaction is posted to the cards application.

Figure 8.2 represents the transaction flow for this scenario.

Scenario 2: Bank B's customer transacting at Bank A's ATM/POS/ online gateway: The transaction is routed to bank A's ATM/POS switch where it is verified that the card is issued by another bank and is from a particular card scheme. Then the transaction is routed to the corresponding card scheme network for further routing to the issuer bank B for authorization and validation. The transaction is confirmed based on the response from the card scheme network. The card scheme is responsible for settlement between the acquiring bank and the issuing bank.

Figure 8.3 represents the transaction flow for this scenario.

Scenario 3: Bank A's customer transacting at bank B's ATM/POS/ online gateway: Bank customers can use the ATM/debit card/credit card issued under a card scheme (like Master or VISA) at any ATM/ POS/online gateway that accepts the card scheme. A customer of Bank A uses the card at an ATM/POS/online gateway acquired by Bank B. This transaction is routed to the ATM/POS switch of Bank B first, which in turn sends this request to the card scheme network for further routing to Bank A. Bank A will validate, post the booking and send back the authorization to the card scheme.

- For ATM/POS transactions, the request is forwarded to the "ATM/ POS authorization server" for validation and authorization. Upon confirmation, the transaction is posted to the accounts/deposits application.

- For credit card transactions, the request is forwarded to the credit card transaction processor for validation and authorization. Upon confirmation, the transaction is posted to the cards application.

Figure 8.4 represents the transaction flow for this scenario.

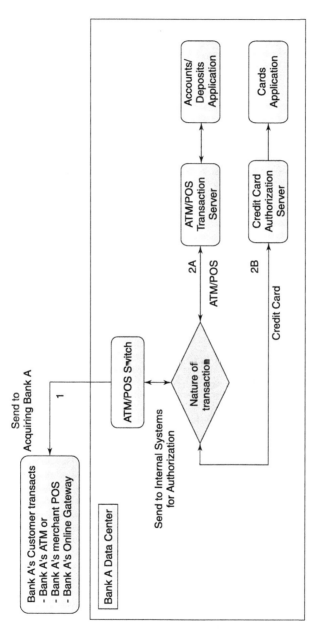

Fig. 8.2 *ATM/POS Transaction — Scenario 1*

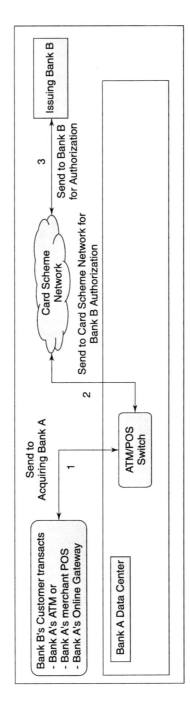

Fig. 8.3 *ATM/POS Transaction — Scenario 2*

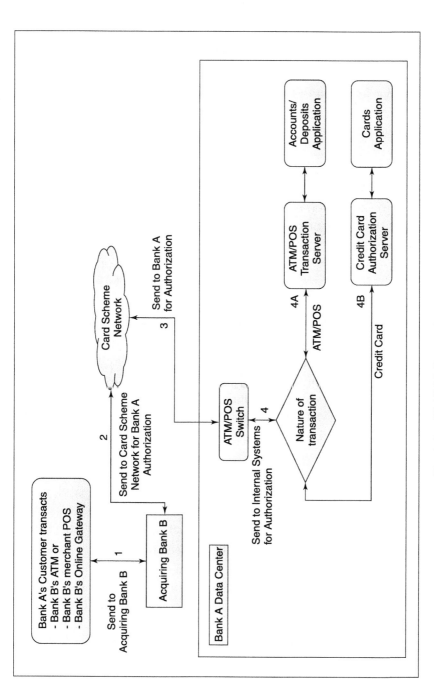

Fig. 8.4 *ATM/POS Transaction — Scenario 3*

ELECTRONIC FUNDS TRANSFER

The electronic funds transfer system allows transfer of funds from a customer's account in one bank to another customer's account in the same bank or another bank electronically. Key players in the electronic funds transfer system and their interactions are described below:

- **Payer:** Instructions are sent by the payers to their bank along with details about the beneficiary bank (as known in the electronic funds transfer system), beneficiary account details (as known to the beneficiary bank), amount and remarks. These instructions may be submitted electronically using the internet banking feature or in the form of paper submission at the branch.

- **Payer's bank:** The payer's bank will validate the instructions and debit the payer's account. If the beneficiary is from the same bank then the bank will credit the beneficiary and alert both parties. However, if the beneficiary is from another participating bank, then the instruction will be routed to the electronic funds transfer system for processing.

- **Electronic funds transfer system:** This is usually facilitated and run by a central bank or national payments association. This system handles electronic funds transfer for low value transactions and performs the settlement in real-time or in one or more batches in a day. All participating banks will be members of the electronic funds transfer system to enable interbank funds movement. The electronic funds transfer system is responsible for transfer of funds from the payer's bank to the payee's bank either on a transaction by transaction basis or a net basis. This system also sends confirmation of the payment to the payer's bank and payee's bank once the settlement is completed.

- **Payee's bank:** The payee's bank will process the payment instructions received from the electronic funds transfer system and post the credit to the payee's account. In case of incorrect account details, the payee's bank will intimate the electronic funds transfer system about the same which will in turn intimate the payer's bank and funds will be returned to the payer.

Figure 8.5 describes the electronic funds transfer process for the payer's bank.

Figure 8.6 describes the electronic funds transfer process for the payee's bank.

DIRECT ENTRY

Direct debit or direct credit allows an organization/institution to process bulk debits or bulk credits for a large customer or employee base having their accounts across multiple banks.

Some examples of direct debits are:

- Telephone company for monthly collection of telephone bills
- Insurance company for regular collection of premiums
- Bank collecting monthly home loan instalments

Some examples of direct credits are:

- Salary credited by corporate houses, directly into employees' accounts
- Credit of dividend directly into investors' accounts by corporate houses
- Tax refunds processed directly into tax payer's accounts

The key players in the processing of direct entry payments are as follows:

- **Organization/Institution:** Institutions that would like to debit or credit a large number of accounts with the appropriate mandate from the account holders. The institution will submit the list of customers, their bank account details, and amount to be debited/credited along with the purpose to the institution's bank. The institution's bank will interface with the direct entry clearing system to process the debits/credits across multiple banks and send the file back to the organization/institution with processing (confirmation/rejection) information for all the records.

- **Institution's bank:** The institution's bank is connected to a direct entry clearing system and will process the requests for direct debits/credits. The institution's bank receives the file from the institution, validates and segregates the file into its own customer debits/credits and those of customers of other banks. Files of other

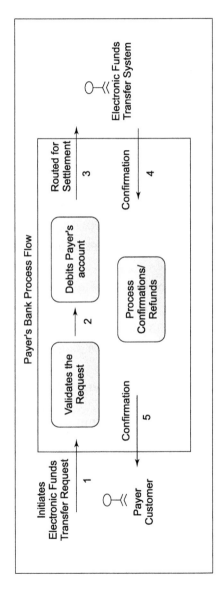

Fig. 8.5 *Electronic Funds Transfer - Payer's Bank Flow*

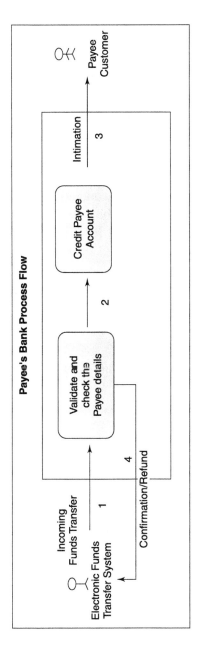

Fig. 8.6 *Electronic Funds Transfer - Payee's Bank Flow*

banks' customers will be sent to the clearing system for further processing.

- **Direct entry clearing system:** This system is usually facilitated and run by a central bank or national payments authority or an independent organization. This system will have all the participating banks as members and will facilitate the movement of information and funds between the institution's bank and multiple customers' banks or vice versa. The files received from the institution's bank will be processed and routed to different banks for processing debits/credits. In the case of direct credits, the clearing system will debit the funds from the institution's bank and credit them to the customer's bank before routing the file to the customer's bank. In the case of direct debit, the clearing system will debit the customer's bank and credit the institution's bank as soon as confirmation of debit is received from the customer's bank.

- **Customer's bank:** The customer's bank is the bank into which direct credits/debits will be posted. The customer's bank will validate the debit/credit requests from the clearing system and verify the customer's mandate before posting the debits to the customer's account.

Key direct entry processes for an institution's bank are presented in Figure 8.7.

Figure 8.8 presents the direct entry processes for a customer's bank.

BILL PAYMENT

A bill payment service enables bank customers to pay their electricity and water bills, insurance premiums, credit card bills etc., using their bank account via internet banking, mobile banking or an ATM. Electronic bill payment helps organizations to significantly improve the receivables and processing costs. It also helps banks in reducing the cash transactions of its customers and switch them to more efficient electronic transactions.

Depending on the infrastructure available in a country, the bill payment services in use are as follows:

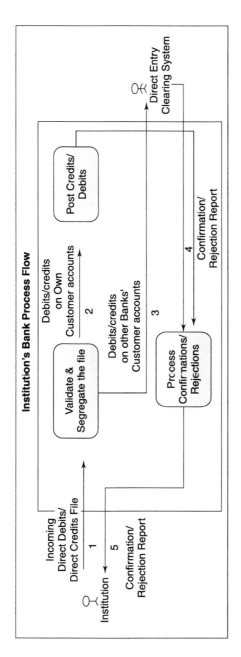

Fig. 8.7 *Direct Entry - Institution's Bank Flow*

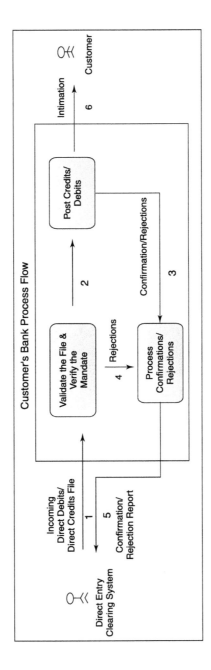

Fig. 8.8 *Direct Entry - Customer's Bank Flow*

- **Centralized billing services:** This service is managed by a centralized service provider that will bring together billing corporations and customer banks on a single platform for bill payment.
- **Direct relationships:** Billing corporations have direct relationships with different banks allowing their customers to register for their bill payment service through their bank.

Figure 8.9 presents a schematic view of the centralized bill payment service provider.

Figure 8.10 presents a schematic view of the billing service through direct relationships.

A billing service through a direct relationship between billers and different banks requires significant investment both on the biller's side to adapt to interface with various banks, as well as on the bank's side to interface with various billers. A centralized billing model is more efficient and standardized and will have improved participation from the market resulting in increased automation in payments.

MOBILE PAYMENTS

In the 'customer channels' section, we discussed the role of the mobile phone as a channel to perform banking transactions. The three broad areas of mobile usage as a channel are:

- SMS banking
- Mobile friendly internet banking
- Mobile App

Using the above options, a mobile phone can be used to access the bank's payment services like payment of bills, transfer of funds, etc. A bank account is mandatory to use these mobile banking features. However, many banks as well as other players like technology companies and mobile network operators are looking at offering mobile based payments on a stand-alone basis. They are looking at ways to gain a share of the market by innovative usage of a mobile phone for banking and payments. These solutions are continuously evolving and vary significantly from market to market. Some of the broad areas of mobile payments are as follows:

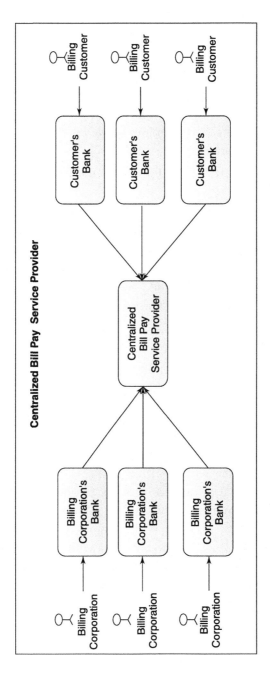

Fig. 8.9 *Centralized Bill Pay Service*

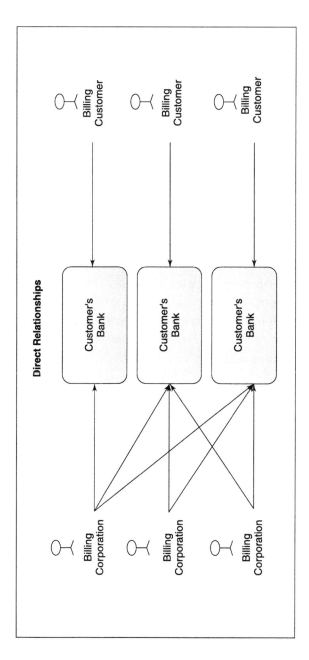

Fig. 8.10 *Bill Pay Service using direct relationships*

- Mobile wallet
- NFC

Mobile Wallet

Banks, financial institutions, technology companies and telecom institutions are looking to offer mobile wallet solutions where funds can be parked, and used for payments as well as withdrawals. The key features of mobile wallet solutions are as follows:

- **KYC:** Mobile wallets may verify the existence of a bank account or credit card of a customer and rely on the KYC conducted as part of opening that account/card. Some of the wallet solutions may have their own KYC procedure at the time of registration via a distributor network.

- **Funding:** Mobile wallets can be funded using a regular bank account, credit/debit cards or by using a distributor network. This means that people can transfer funds into their mobile wallet from their bank account, credit card or pay at the distributor. Some of the wallets offered by telecom companies offer to fund the mobile wallet from the mobile balance that enables them to leverage the wide distribution network they have built for mobile services.

- **Funds transfer:** Mobile wallets offer various options for transfer of funds, as follows:
  - **Bill payment to registered billers:** Funds will be debited from the wallet and credited to the billers' accounts.
  - **Person-to-person payments using the mobile number:** Funds will be debited from the payer's wallet and credited to the payee's wallet.
  - **Person-to-merchant payments:** Funds will be debited from the payer's wallet and credited to the merchant account. The merchant can be identified by a merchant number or QR code scanning at the time of payment.

- **Withdrawal:** Funds in a mobile wallet can be withdrawn using the following options:
  - **Withdraw funds into a bank account:** Funds will be debited from the wallet and credited into the customer's bank account.

- **Withdraw at an ATM:** Some ATMs have the capability to offer card-less withdrawal of money using an SMS based code. Wallets can utilize these features to offer withdrawal at ATMs using an SMS.

Features and target customers of mobile wallets vary significantly. Some of the providers are using mobile wallets to gain a share of the market in electronic payments and are offering high end features. On the other hand simple solutions along with distribution networks are built to address the 'un-banked' or 'under-banked' segment and help financial inclusion in the process.

Near Field Communication (NFC)

The credit card is the most widely used customer identification, credit and payment mode, combined all-in-one product. Usage of a card at merchant locations typically involves swiping the card at the merchant locations, entering the PIN or signing the transaction slip. This is a high touch process and hence the need for a contact-less and faster transaction at point-of-sale. Near Field Communication (NFC) technology allows merchants' POS devices to read the card or mobile details at the tap, and low value transactions can be cleared without any additional PIN or signature. Mobiles embedded with NFC readable chips can be used as an alternate to carrying plastic cards to transact at merchant locations.

PAYMENTS TECHNOLOGY

Having looked at the various retail payment options and message flows, let us look at the retail payments technology. As discussed earlier, typical retail payment instruments are cheques, cards, electronic funds transfer, bill payments, mobile payments and direct debit/credit payments. These payment instruments were introduced over a period of time, and this is also reflected in the way payments technology has evolved in the banks. Typically, banks with legacy payments technology have different payment processing applications for different payment instruments.

Figure 8.11 depicts the legacy payments technology landscape.

Key components of payments technology are described below.

Payment Initiation Channel

Payment channel applications are used by a payer, payee or bank staff to initiate a payment in the system. Cheque payment is typically initiated by the payments operations team at the back office by either manually or automatically capturing the cheque details in the system for clearing. The latest scanning technology enables payee customers to directly capture the cheque details at an ATM or using a mobile banking application.

Electronic funds transfer can be initiated through a branch with the help of the branch staff or through online/mobile banking directly by the customers. Online/Mobile banking allows customers to create standing instructions for periodic payments. Such standing instructions are captured within an online banking application which in turn will generate payment instructions on behalf of the customer at the periodicity specified by customer. Mobile payments are initiated by the payer/payee using their mobile app or mobile wallet.

Direct entry payments are generated based on the direct entry credit or debit file received from the clearing institution. Based on the feed from the crediting/debiting organization, a direct debit or credit file, generated by the bank for its own customers, will also feed into the direct entry payment processing application.

Bill payment initiation depends on the bill payment solution available in the market. In markets with a centralized bill payment provider, bill payment is initiated by the file received from such a provider. For the billers signed up with them, banks will receive the file from the billers directly. This file will be segregated into own customer transactions ("on us") and other bank transactions. "On us" transactions will be routed to internal systems for processing whereas other bank transactions are sent to a clearing organization. All the bill payments generated are presented to the customer in an online banking application for consent. All the consented payments will be posted for booking.

Payment Processing Applications

Payment processing applications handle various functions related to transaction processing. Banks with legacy payments technology

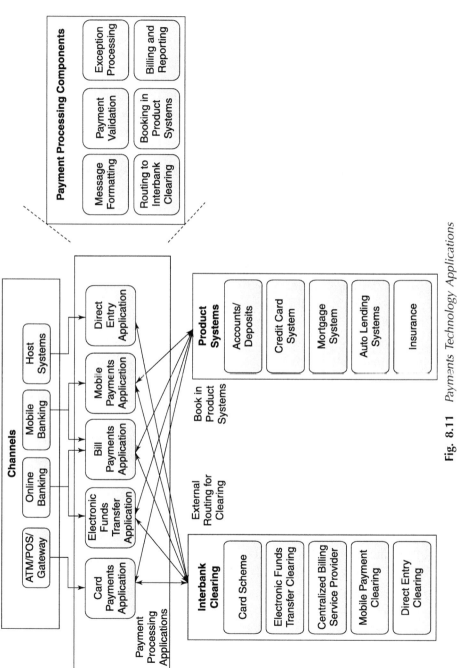

Fig. 8.11 *Payments Technology Applications*

will have different applications for different payment instruments but handling broadly the same functions listed below.

- **Message formatting:** Incoming payment messages from different channels have different formats; similarly all the messages to external entities like clearing institutions have to follow certain pre-defined formats. In the case of file based inputs, file formats, header, footer and sequence are pre-defined. This component handles conversion of incoming message formats to an internal format for processing. This component also converts an internal format to an external format before sending the messages out to clearing institutions or customers.

- **Payment validation:** Incoming payment instructions have to be validated for customer, account, limits, sanctions etc. Some examples for validations are: "Account is not frozen", "Daily transaction limit not reached" etc. Instructions that do not meet validation criteria may be rejected or set aside for manual intervention by the operations team depending on the validation failure.

- **Exception processing:** This component allows the operations team to act on payment exceptions that have resulted as part of validation. Users will be able to override the errors and initiate the processing or reject the payment instructions after verifying the details.

- **Interbank clearing interface:** This component enables payment applications to interface with clearing systems for interbank payments. This component also processes the response from the clearing system and updates payment records accordingly.

- **Products systems interface:** This component enables payment applications to interface with product systems to post the bookings related to various payment instructions. Payments will be booked into accounts/deposits, credit card or lending systems to update the balances accordingly. Posting the booking in a product system may happen in real time or in batch, depending on the technology capability and nature of payments.

- **Billing and reporting:** This component enables computation of the charges for payment instructions for its customers. This component will collect the payments transaction data and apply the charging rules to arrive at the pricing. This components also provides payment related reporting either in the form of an e-mail, SMS or a letter depending on the type of transaction and account configuration.

The legacy payments technology landscape has significant disadvantages in terms of time-to-market, cost of maintenance and system complexity. Due to the duplication of several payment related processes across different applications for different instruments, the cost of maintenance of such legacy payments technology is very high. A number of banks are moving to a payments hub architecture either in total or for part of their payments requirements. A payments hub encapsulates all the payment processes across instruments and provides a configurable system for different types of instruments. There are a number of market products available in the payments area to support the "payments hub" architecture. Payments hub solutions offer simplification of application landscape, scalability, faster time-to-market and cost savings.

Figure 8.12 depicts the payments hub architecture.

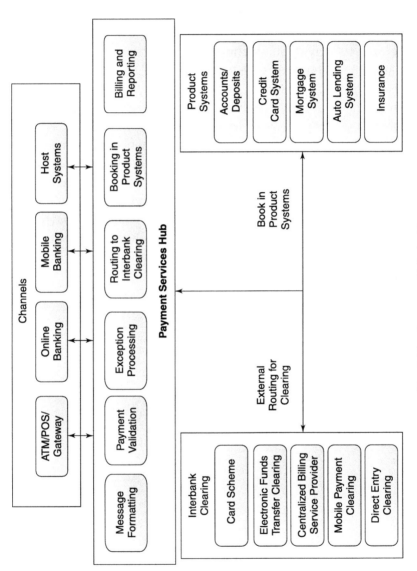

Fig. 8.12 *Payments Hub Architecture*

CHAPTER 9
Enterprise Systems

Apart from the customer facing functions, there are number of horizontal support functions at the corporate level that are essential. Enterprise systems address the needs of the corporate functions of a bank. Corporate functions are typically located in head/regional offices and do not handle customer transactions on a day-to-day basis. Let us look at some of the key functions, their role and IT needs at the corporate level.

CHIEF EXECUTIVE OFFICER

The chief executive officer and his leadership team are responsible for the successful management and growth of the bank. They are responsible for setting up the strategic direction for the bank, overall focus areas, product strategy, risk management etc. It is important for them to have a management overview of the various parameters of the bank's operations. This information needs to be provided across products, customer segments, branches and regions.

CHIEF FINANCIAL OFFICER

The chief financial officer and his team are responsible for financial operations including financial budgeting, cost management, financial statements and tax processing. This team will require finance and account systems to manage the financial operations.

SALES AND MARKETING

Sales and marketing personnel are responsible for building the brand, running promotional campaigns, customer analytics etc. This team will interact with various business/product heads to run the specific campaigns online and offline to promote sales. This team will require IT systems that enable them to run the campaigns and measure the efficiency, capture the leads, manage customer segmentation and customer analytics.

HEAD OF HUMAN RESOURCES

He/She is responsible for the personnel in the banking operations. Recruiting the best talent, nurturing them and retaining them are the key functions of the human resources team. Some of the IT needs of the human resource team are workforce management, payroll processing, talent management, knowledge management etc.

HEAD OF RISK MANAGEMENT

The head of risk management is responsible for setting up risk management policies, and monitoring and controlling the risks. IT needs of the risk management team are risk monitoring, risk control and reporting.

In the rest of this chapter, we will look at some of the important enterprise applications.

CRM SYSTEMS

Typically, market standard Customer Relationship Management (CRM) systems offer the marketing, sales and service features required for a bank. These features are provided to the bank staff through indirect channels like a branch, call centre, operations etc. CRM systems broadly cover the following functions:

- **Marketing:** To design, plan and execute the campaign programs to promote the bank's products like credit cards, mortgages etc. The campaign can be targeted to existing customers, or to a particular segment of potential customers. Effectiveness of a campaign will be tracked closely, based on the leads generated and converted successfully.
- **Sales:** All the leads generated through various marketing campaigns will be followed up as potential opportunities for the next steps like sales, filling up application forms and further origination steps.
- **Service:** All service requests/complaints from existing customers are captured in this component and tracked for effective closure. Banks will also have service history information for future reference.

Table 9.1 Sales and Marketing Applications-Snapshot

Actors	The marketing team will use this application to create and manage campaigns, maintain customer lists, manage the contents on websites, maintain product brochures etc.
	The sales team will use this application to convert the leads, provide additional information and sign up customers by getting the applications forms.
	Service/Operations staff at a branch and call-centre will use this application to view/capture service requests, customer contact history.
Interfaces	This application interfaces with the customer master for customers' profiles and details.
	This application is integrated with indirect channels and customer channels to offer the services.
	This application interfaces with external data providers to receive the "prospects list" to run promotional campaigns.
	This application interfaces with DW/BI systems to feed data on campaigns, leads/opportunities and service requests.
	This application also interfaces with product origination systems to process the filled in application forms, once sale is completed.
Key data	The following key data will be maintained in this application:
	Campaigns: Information like the duration of the campaign, target prospects, mode of campaigns, budgets etc.
	Leads/Opportunities: Information like potential customer opportunities, product, timeline of the opportunity.
	Service requests: Information about service requests like customer details, requests, products, fulfilment time etc.
	Contact summary: Customer contact summary during the sales process.

Relationship managers at branches/call centre staff will be able to get a view of the history of the service requests and will be able to assist customers in a better fashion.

Figure 9.1 presents an overview of IT systems for sales, service and marketing team. As described above some of these components are typically implemented by off-the-shelf CRM applications.

The application components are described below.

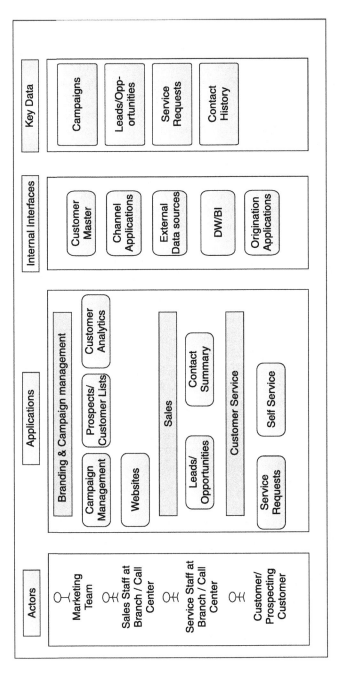

Fig. 9.1 *Marketing Applications*

BRAND & CAMPAIGN MANAGEMENT

Campaign management: This application component will be used by the marketing team to manage campaigns online or offline. Campaigns can be for specific products, for a specific duration with a goal to increase the awareness on the product and sign-up customers for that product. It is also important for the bank to know the effectiveness of the campaign across customer segments. A campaign can be run for a section of existing customers or for new prospects. Campaign management features include creating a campaign plan, creating the necessary collateral, running the campaign and capturing all the leads coming out of the campaign with a potential timeline.

Marketing conducts various campaigns related to the bank's products and offerings to the general public over various channels. Some examples of marketing campaigns to the general public are:

- Google Adwords campaign for searches on mortgages in a particular city or group of cities
- A stall at a popular trade fair
- E-mail campaign for a given profile of prospective customers
- Advertisements in popular financial daily papers about wealth management products

Most of these campaigns are conducted with the campaign partner but are tracked and managed within the bank in terms of campaign duration, budget, target customers, expected/actual number of leads, ROI etc.

Prospect/Customer lists: Banks may tie up with third party data providers/partners for contact information of people with certain defined profiles. This information will be used as part of generic campaigns like e-mail, SMS and telephone calls.

Apart from general campaigns, banks may run campaigns for their existing customers to increase the revenue per customer. It is lot cheaper to sell a product to an existing customer, than to acquire a new customer.

Some examples of campaigns targeted towards customers are:

Generic mailer campaign with credit card offers for all customers who have been associated with the bank for more than three years with an average balance above a threshold, but who are not currently availing of credit card services.

Targeted relevant offers to customers based on profile, transaction history and banking relationship.

For customer mailer campaigns, the marketing team will require customer lists and contact details matching various criteria like net worth, products, relationship with the bank and customer profile etc. Depending on the mode of the campaign, the customer's name and address details will be sent to the mailing department for posting the collateral, or e-mail ids will be used for bulk mailing.

- **Customer analytics:** Performing advanced analytics is one of the options to generate targeted customer campaigns. As part of its services to its customers, banks have access to a lot of information about customers, such as income profile, expense profile, life stage, customer locations, purchase patterns etc. Advanced analytics on customer data history will provide insights into customers' future needs. These needs can be converted to targeted offers and sent to customers via online, mail, telephone or SMS channels.

- **Websites:** Bank websites were discussed in the section on customer channels in this book. A bank's website provides an opportunity for branding as well as distribution of product information/brochures. The marketing team is responsible for the content of the website and will typically use a content management system for creation, review and publishing of the content.

SALES

- **Leads/Opportunities:** This application component maintains details of potential prospects/existing customers who are in need of one or more banking products. All the leads are typically mapped to a marketing campaign so that the effectiveness and ROI of a campaign can be tracked. All the leads from various campaigns will be collected, consolidated and further routed to the appropriate sales team to close the sales process. This involves calling, sending letters with special offers to customers, providing clarifications on products, getting the application form filled up and initiating origination.

- **Contact summary:** This application maintains the customer's contact summary during a sales process to enable completion of sale.

CUSTOMER SERVICE

- **Service requests:** There are multiple channels through which customers are serviced like branches, call centres and also self-service channels like internet banking and mobile phones. Customer service requests like change of address, change of contact details, product clarifications etc., will be provided through these channels. This application will be used to keep track of all the customer service requests and route them to the appropriate team for closure. A history of service requests is maintained for future tracking as well as getting insights into customer service patterns.
- **Self-service:** Some of the service requests can be offered as self-service tools and can be completely serviced without any intervention of branch/operations staff. Some examples are requests for cheque books, cancelling a cheque book, account statements etc. These self-service tools are accessible through customer channels like online and mobile banking.

DATA WAREHOUSE AND BUSINESS INTELLIGENCE

Data are an important asset for any organization especially for banks as their entire business revolves around information. Banks' core systems are designed for executing efficient, high performance transactions to meet stringent customer response times. However, banks' information requirements need to process much larger volumes of data to arrive at summary trends and management information. The goal of the data warehouse is to capture the transaction data in a historical form that can be used to arrive at summary information, trends and advanced analytics. Transaction systems like core products that are optimized for update are called fully normalized whereas data warehouse systems capture the historical data in a query friendly format for analytical processing.

Broadly, usage of data can be classified under the following heads:

- **Operational summary reports:** Management will need operational summary reports detailing weekly, monthly, quarterly and annual business performance across various parameters like branches, regions, products and customer segments. These reports are used in reviewing the performance of various units in terms of volume of business, growth etc., on an ongoing basis.

- **Regulatory reports:** Regulators require various reports from banks across their operations to monitor compliance to various regulations and also monitor the overall health of the banking system. Apart from pre-defined reports, regulators will also require ad-hoc reports from time-to-time. Banks should be able to comply with these regulatory requirements with accurate and timely reports.

- **Analytics:** Banks can use the historical information to arrive at key decisions like monitoring fraud, cross-sell opportunities, customer behavioural scoring etc. Analytical information from various subject areas like customers, accounts and products, needs to be consolidated and reported. Some examples are customer profiling, scoring and profitability. A data warehouse provides underlying data to build analytical models and analytics enables usage of historical data to arrive at business decisions/raise alerts.

Bank's corporate functions have varying requirements on the data warehouse system, for example information needs of marketing and risk functions are significantly different. Data warehouses should ideally be built with a broad scope of enterprise requirements in mind with a universe of all the data requirements. But in reality banks face a number of challenges in their data warehouse implementations as mentioned below:

Table 9.2 Data Warehouse and Business Intelligence Applications-Snapshot

Actors	Banks management teams dealing with various functions like strategy, sales, marketing, risk management, finance and operations will access the reports from the data warehouse/ business intelligence solution. Reports to regulators are generated out of this application. Analytics applications will use the data warehouse for data mining and modelling.
Interfaces	This application interfaces with customer master, all product systems, enterprise applications like finance, HR and CRM to extract the relevant data.
Key data	The following key data are stored in this application: - Operational data store contains the aggregated transaction data from all the sources. These data store contain key and relevant information about the transactions. - Aggregated data stored in the form of dimensions and facts for subject areas like customers, accounts, products. - Cubes built from dimensional data for analytical processing and reporting.

- Evolution of an existing data warehouse solution over a period of time leaving point solutions for various business needs without an integrated approach to the data warehouse.
- Legacy technologies for data extraction, transformation and loading.
- Usage of multiple technologies by multiple departments, e.g., different reporting tools
- Mergers and acquisitions related system integration leave out comprehensive integration of data warehouse systems due to costs and complexities involved.

Figure 9.2 presents an overview of data warehouse/business intelligence application.

Key application components are described below.

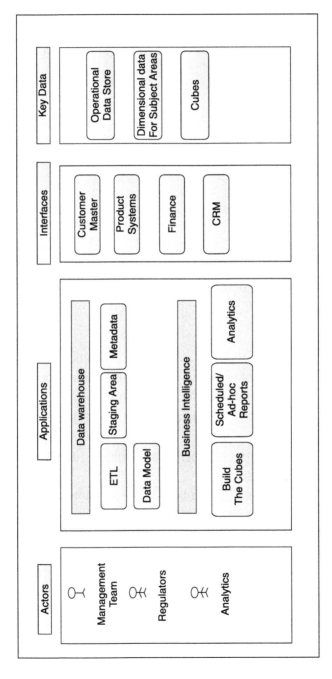

Fig. 9.2   *Data Warehouse/BI Applications*

Data Warehouse

This component mainly covers the extraction of data from source systems, cleansing the data, transforming the data and loading it to the data warehouse. The sub-components are as follows:

- **Extract-Transform-Load (ETL):** As a first step, the ETL process extracts the data from various source systems like accounts/ deposits, credit cards, mortgages etc. For large banks, there may be multiple systems handling the same function depending on the geography. Extracted data are validated, cleansed and transformed to the target state in multiple stages. These data will then be loaded on to the data warehouse system.

- **Staging areas:** Data received from the various systems are stored in the staging area for processing and validation before they are loaded into the data warehouse. This includes bringing the data from across multiple sources to a consistent format like data values (status codes) and data formats (number formats). Also, data from the source system is transformed to the target state dimensional data model in multiple stages, by incrementally aggregating the data at each stage.

- **Metadata:** Data from various systems are extracted, cleansed and loaded into the data warehouse, usually in multi-stage processing. Every attribute in a data warehouse has its roots in one of the source systems, but is transformed and cleansed. Metadata will maintain the data mapping from the source system to target systems, and all the validations and transformations that happen during the process. Metadata is an important tool to validate data quality.

- **Data model:** The data model for the data warehouse solution is typically based on dimensional modelling. Different business entities such as customers, products and accounts are called subject areas. Each subject area has several facts, e.g., accounts has balance, transaction amount etc. Each fact has several dimensions, for example the loan account balance can be characterized by several dimensions such as product type, day/ month/year, customer type and branch etc. The dimensional data model has all the facts and corresponding dimensions in the form of star schema. The dimensional data model does not include any transactional attributes like account number, customer id etc.

Figure 9.3 presents a sample star schema diagram for loan balance.

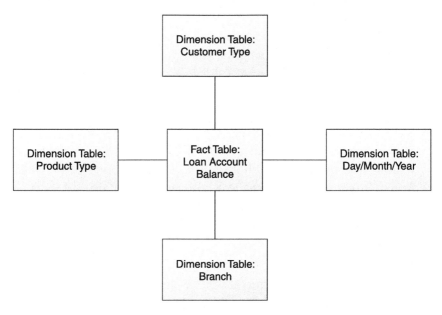

Fig. 9.3 *Sample Star Schema*

Such a dimensional data model allows for easy slicing and dicing of data and aggregation to enable easy analytical processing of data.

A data model for banks is commercially available in the market along with the necessary analytical reporting catering to various business scenarios.

Business Intelligence

This component covers analytical processing and reporting of data in the data warehouse.

- **Build the cubes:** A cube can be seen as a fact or business attribute of a subject area that is represented in multiple dimensions. A cube is designed based on analytical/reporting needs and cubes are populated from the data warehouse typically using ETL technology. For example, loan distributions from the dimension of calendar months, branch and product types. Several customized reports can be setup on such cubes and also ad-hoc reports can be generated.

- **Scheduled/Ad-hoc reports:** The BI reporting tool allows for configuration of the various scheduled reports based on the cube design. These reporting tools provide an intuitive user interface to design various dash boards and charts to visually represent the aggregate information and trends. Reports can be scheduled at specified times during the day or an on-demand basis and can be delivered over various channels like e-mail, web, mobile and tablet applications.

- **Analytics:** Advanced analytics can be run on the data warehouse to arrive at a business decision or to raise alerts. Analytics tools enable one to capture the analytical models to identify various business events/alerts. These models can be run on the historical data to derive deep insights from the historical data. For example, arriving at potential cross-selling opportunities for the existing customers, based on the historical product usage of similar customers.

HUMAN RESOURCES

Employees are the key to any industry and in particular are very critical for a knowledge oriented industry like banking. Attracting and retaining a good team and helping them grow in the organization will be a key differentiator for any bank. Human resources is typically an independent department reporting directly to the CEO of the bank.

HR systems cater to the needs of the human resource management department and key applications are depicted in Figure 9.4.

Table 9.3 HR Applications-Snapshot

Actors	HR managers will use this application for various HR processes like recruitment, on-boarding, performance management, pay-roll processing etc.
	Recruitment agencies potentially interact with this application to support recruitment, timesheet submission and payroll processing.
	Employees will use this application for timesheets, performance management and pay roll details.
Interfaces	This application interfaces with indirect channels for taking on new employees (on-boarding) with appropriate authentication and authorization.
	This application interfaces with the payments application and finance application for processing the pay-roll.
Key data	This application maintains the employee master records for the bank, employee competency and performance details. Timesheet and payroll data are also maintained in this application.

Key application components are described below.

On-boarding

- **Recruitment/Hiring:** This application caters to the recruitment/ hiring needs of the bank. It supports publishing of open requirements, receiving potential candidates' applications, evaluation and confirmation of the selected candidates. This application may interface with potential recruitment agencies and social media.

- **Induction:** The employee induction process involves creating a master record for new employees, setting up the appropriate salary structure, providing access to various office facilities, and providing them access to all the indirect channel applications needed to perform their job. There are a multitude of systems for which access needs to be given and at the same time access should only be restricted to the applications and functions which the employee is authorized to access. Another feature that is typically implemented is single-sign on using which one time login credentials are passed on to different applications so that the user does not have to login every time.

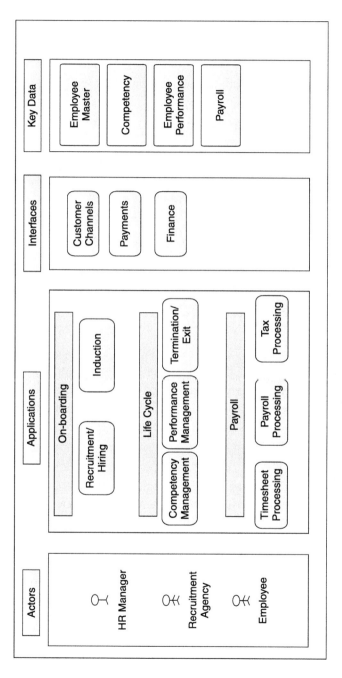

Fig. 9.4 *HR Applications*

Life Cycle

- **Competency management:** This component enables HR managers to track the competency levels of the employees and plan their career progression. HR managers will be able identify the competency gaps in the bank at present, as well as the bank's future needs and plan accordingly.

- **Performance management:** This component enables measurement and tracking of employee performance against set objectives and targets. It digitizes the employee performance over a period of time and enables HR managers to take necessary measures in case of poor performance.

- **Termination/Exit:** Employee attrition, either voluntary or involuntary, is a concern for HR managers. This component can be used to analyze the root cause for employee attrition, so that necessary corrective action can be taken. This application also supports the termination process that includes financial settlement, revoking user access etc.

Payroll

- **Timesheet processing:** Timesheets for employees and contractors provide very good insights into the bank's operations as well as providing the basis for payroll processing. This component enables capturing necessary timesheets as per the bank's requirements.

- **Payroll processing:** This system processes all the payroll benefits to employees and contractors. This system needs to address multiple currencies and country specific roles in case of staff distributed across multiple countries. Employee pay slips are generated and distributed through various channels. Payroll processing interfaces with the payments application and finance application for processing payments and accounting.

- **Tax processing:** This is a sub-component of pay-roll processing and manages the tax processing at source and tax payments to authorities. This component will have in-built rules for multiple countries in case of a distributed workforce.

FINANCE & ACCOUNTING

Finance and accounting applications enable the finance department of the bank to manage the general ledger, accounting, payables, receivables and financial statements. Some of the standard functions that are supported by these systems are:

- Managing the general ledger and accounting as per the chart of accounts.
- Publishing financial statements quarterly and annually, including the income statement, cash flow statement and balance sheet.
- Managing accounts payables to vendors and receivables from customers.
- Tax processing of financial transactions.
- Managing cash flows.
- Managing fixed assets.

Figure 9.5 gives an overview of the finance and accounts applications.

Table 9.4 Finance Applications-Snapshot

Actors	The finance and accounting department of the bank predominantly uses this system for all finance operations. The procurement team accesses this system to track accounts payable to vendors. Auditors access this system for auditing the financial transactions and results.
Interfaces	All product systems feed this application with accounts and transaction information for posting. This application feeds the data warehouse/BI system with the general ledger and accounts data for consolidation of historical data and generating reports.
Key data	This application maintains the following key data General ledger – Chart of accounts and transactions on the accounts Accounts – Accounts payable and accounts receivable Assets – All fixed assets of the bank

Application components are described below.

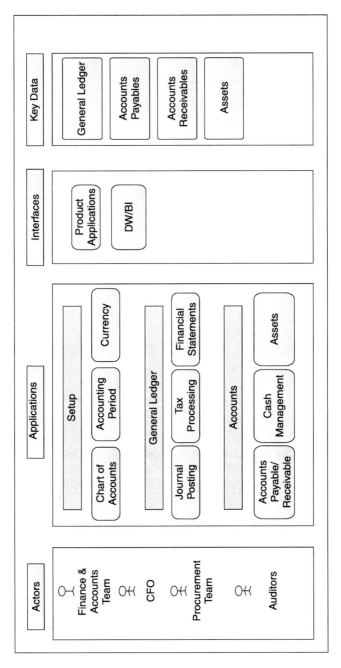

Fig. 9.5 *Finance Applications*

Setup

- **General Ledger (GL) chart of accounts:** The GL chart of accounts is the master data and it refers to the bank's accounting structure required for financial reporting (e.g., region, branch etc.,) and all the bank accounts will be aligned to the accounting organizational structure. Accounts are also classified into various categories as "P & L account", "capital account" etc. All the bookings performed in core applications will be processed according to the GL hierarchy and posted in the GL.

- **Accounting period:** The accounting period is defined in the finance application. All the transactions are aggregated within an accounting period. The accounting period will be closed once all the financial statements are generated and approved.

- **Currencies:** Bank transactions take place in multiple currencies and these will be processed in the GL. Currency conversion happens to report transactions in a single currency. Acceptable currencies and their exchange rates are defined in this component.

General Ledger

- **Journal posting:** Journal posting is an interface and processing intensive application as all the product systems will pass the booking transactions via data loads. Once all the transactions are loaded, then accounting rules are applied to post them on to the general ledger. Posting will take into consideration the accounting rules typically defined by central banks for revenue recognition, NPAs, provisions etc.

- **Tax processing:** Tax computations have to be carried out as part of transaction posting and overall tax liability has to be arrived at for the accounting period. Tax payment processing and necessary tax file reports to be generated are handled in this process.

- **Financial statements:** At the end of the accounting period, financial statements will need to be generated based on the various bookings posted on to the general ledger. For global banks listed in multiple countries, financial statements have to be generated in multiple accounting standards. Also, there are regulatory requirements related to the format of the financial statements which need to be complied with.

Accounts

- **Accounts payable:** Banks will have large procurement divisions to make all the necessary purchases for the bank. The procurement module will have features for ordering a set of products from a preferred supplier list and also provision for suppliers to raise invoices. Purchase orders, vendor invoices and vendor payments will be captured in the accounts payable module and tracked to closure.

  Accounts receivables tracks the receivables due from customers against the payments received from them.

- **Cash management:** This component handles the cash flow projections in terms of incoming cash flow as well as outgoing cash flow projections to arrive at cash planning and management.

- **Fixed assets:** This application component is used to manage the fixed assets of a bank and their book value. Fixed assets can be office equipment, vehicles, technical infrastructure etc. This application will have features like capturing the assets at the time of purchase, valuations, depreciations and finally retirements.

TREASURY, RISK AND COMPLIANCE

The most important activity of a bank, next only to collecting deposits and funding loans, is risk management. Efficient risk management is the single difference between successful banks and banks that have collapsed. The risk management function is a combination of art, science, instinct, execution as well as a bit of luck, all combined in one. Banks face a number of risks and these risks have to be measured and monitored strictly according to the risk management policy of the bank. Banks are one of the highly regulated industries and they have strict regulatory and reporting requirements to comply with. Banks rely significantly on the technology for risk management as well as compliance. Table 9.5 identifies some of the key risks faced by banks and the possible mitigation measures put in place by them.

Table 9.5 Risk Management

Risk	Description	Mitigation Measures
Credit risk	It is the risk of a borrower unwilling or unable to pay the interest or principal or both	• Thorough credit appraisal at the time of origination including verifying the past history in the form of credit scoring • Risk based pricing that charges products at a premium for high risk customers • Credit monitoring through regular collection of information, statistical analysis etc., and taking the necessary corrective measures
Credit concentration risk	The risk of problems with one country or a group of countries or industries causing significant losses to the bank	• Defining limits at the country, group and industry segments and tracking all the credits against the pre-defined limits • Periodic monitoring of limits and necessary corrective actions
Interest rate & liquidity risk	Bank deposits are usually held for a shorter duration than high value lending products. Interest rate risk is the risk of deposit rates going up compared to committed long term loans at lower rates. Liquidity risk is the inability of the bank to able to honour deposits due to non-liquidity of the long term assets (loans)	• Strict monitoring of the asset liability mismatch across various time periods • Optimal ratio of fixed interest vs. variable interest loans based on the interest rate forecast • Interest rate swap agreements that enable banks to swap fixed interest rate proceeds with variable rate proceeds or vice versa

Operational risk	It is the risk of an intentional/ unintentional error in the operations causing major losses for the bank. For example, service deficiency or missing a payment deadline etc.	• Well defined operational procedures and guidelines • Digitization of operational processes and monitoring of critical deadlines • Maker/Checker implementation for filtering out data entry errors for key information • Segregation of duties and work practices, and guidelines to prevent any malpractices

Treasury is another critical function of a bank that plays an important role in managing some of the critical risks of the bank like interest rate risk, liquidity risk, FOREX risk etc. This department closely monitors various parameters related to these risks and proactively enters into financial agreements to mitigate these risks. The treasury is also responsible for deploying surplus funds of the bank to be able to generate additional revenues. Treasury and risk management functions cut across retail, corporate divisions of the banks, and further details on technology architecture for these functions will be elaborated in Part 3 of this series, which focuses on "Corporate Banking". However, in this chapter we give an overview of the technology related to credit risk management.

Credit risk management is about right credit appraisal at the time of origination, continuous monitoring of the credit and an effective collections process in case of bad debts. Analytics based scoring is one of the critical components of credit risk management technology at each phase of the credit life cycle.

- **At the time of origination:** Application scoring based on various sources of input including a credit score to arrive at the credit decision, to arrive at the credit limit and also to arrive at the pricing based on the risk.

- **During the life of the credit:** Use of analytics to arrive at behavioural scoring of the customer based on various sources of data including all transactions within the bank. Having a single customer view of data and aggregation of transactions based on the single customer data is very important to be able to capture customer behaviour. Behavioural scoring can be used to proactively take mitigation measures like reduction of limits.

- **Bad debt collections:** Analytics can be used to arrive at the best collections strategy and helps to deploy resources efficiently for the collections process.

CHAPTER 10
Integration

In the earlier chapters, we have looked at three broad categories of retail banking applications:

- Channel applications
- Products applications
- Enterprise applications

Typically, a medium to large bank's technology landscape will have hundreds of applications across multiple technologies. These applications have a complex web of interfaces and data flows between them to provide the necessary functionality. It is important to design the interfaces carefully to make sure that there is less coupling between the applications. In other words, it should be possible to enhance/modify the business logic in an application without mandatorily having to modify all the applications that interface with it. Less coupling also helps from an organization's perspective. Typically, IT organizations are very large and different units will be operating a different group of applications and hence strong coupling will involve excessive dependencies between IT units. Finally the technical nature of the interface like real-time, batch etc., should be designed based on the nature of interactions between the applications.

Some interfaces that are established between different banking systems are given below.

MESSAGE BASED INTEGRATION

Message based integration is inherently asynchronous in nature and provides the maximum decoupling at the run-time between the invoking and invoked application. The invoking application will prepare the service request and place it in the input queue of the invoked application for processing. The invoked application will pick up the input records for processing and place the result in the output queue for consumption of the invoking application. The invoking application can place its request even if the invoked application is not active and vice versa and hence provides maximum decoupling at the run time. It is also possible to implement a synchronous service using message based integration.

Figure 10.1 presents a schematic view of message based integration.

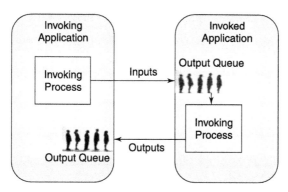

Fig. 10.1 *Message Based Integration*

Some examples of message based integration are:

- Interfaces between the payments module and other product systems
- Customer master processing of new customer records added to the cards system

FILE BASED INTEGRATION

This approach is best suited for large data based batch interface between applications. The invoking application will prepare the file with the records to be processed and will make it available for the invoked application for processing. The invoked application will process all the records in the file and prepare the output file with the results/errors. The output file will optionally be made available to the invoking application for further processing.

Figure 10.2 presents a schematic view of file based integration.

Some examples of file based integration are given below.

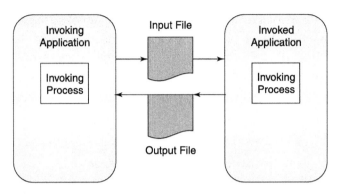

Fig. 10.2 *File Based Integration*

- Product systems feeding transaction data to the finance application
- Direct entry payments processing
- Bill payment feeds

DATA INTEGRATION

Extract-Transform-Load (ETL) is the most commonly used data integration technique. ETL is the process of fetching data from the source system, validating and transforming the data as required by the target system and loading it to the target database.

Figure 10.3 presents a schematic view of ETL based integration.

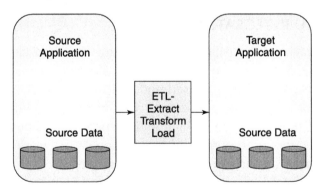

Fig. 10.3 *ETL Based Integration*

Some of the examples of ETL are:

- Finance application feeding GL data to the data warehouse application
- Product systems feeding transaction data to the data warehouse application

SERVICE BASED INTEGRATION (SOA)

Service based integration is one of the mechanisms to modernize the application landscape without losing the business logic in legacy applications. Business logic in the application is exposed via standard interfaces as "services" for use by other applications. The level of functionality embedded in each of these services is a key design parameter and is generally referred to as granularity. It is important to have the right granularity to ensure that services are not too big or too small for any practical use. Also, service oriented architecture will enable an efficient configuration of the service with minimal dependencies between the invoking application and the invoked application.

Figure 10.4 presents a schematic view of service based integration.

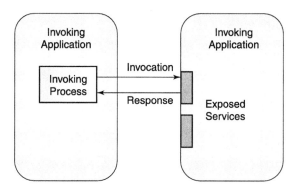

Fig. 10.4 *Service Based Integration*

Some examples of service based integration are:

- Call centre application invoking service for extracting customers' details

- Teller application invoking the service to check the balance in an account

PROCESS INTEGRATION (BPM)

Process integration is about aligning IT applications to business processes. IT applications are typically designed for product requirements (like core banking, payments, cards etc.), or are designed based on the functional domain (like channels, CRM, finance etc.) However, a business process will have several process steps and cuts across the applications. A business process may also have manual steps (like manually authorizing overdrafts above a certain amount) in between the automatic process steps.

A BPM suite of applications allows users to capture the business processes in the form of modelling (BPM) the process steps. These process steps can be implemented in the run time in the form of Business Process Execution Language (BPEL). Each transaction goes through various process steps to produce the desired outcome. Business transactions pending at various steps can be monitored by managers using Business Activity Monitoring (BAM) and necessary corrective actions can be taken. An example of process integration is the origination process that cuts across various applications across different departments.

Figure 10.5 presents an overview of the sample business process orchestration using BPM.

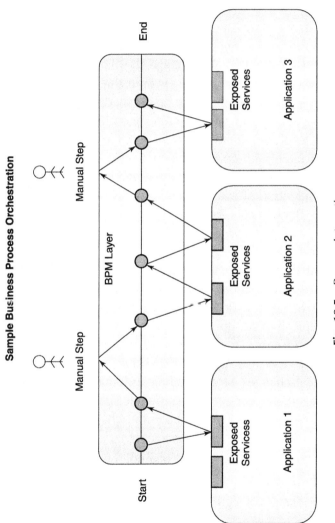

Fig. 10.5 *Process Integration*

CHAPTER 11
Transformation Programs

A bank's systems landscape and technology continuously change and evolve to meet emerging business demands. IT budgets divided between "Run the Bank" and "Change the Bank" form a significant portion of overall costs for a bank. Within the technology divisions, "Run the Bank" refers to the costs associated with maintaining the banking applications and infrastructure according to the availability and service level requirements. "Change the Bank" refers to the changes associated with enhancements to the application to cater to business demands related to expansion, efficiency or compliance. It is the strategic intention of every technology division of a bank to keep the "Run the Bank" costs lower and at the same time improve the service levels, stability and availability of the applications. This allows more time and a larger budget for "Change the Bank" programs that can help banks generate additional revenue, improve customers' experience, reduce manual efforts or comply with regulations. In this chapter, we will look at some of the large change programs that banks typically take up. Due to the very nature of the complex application landscape, managing large change programs can be a challenging task for banks. Executive sponsorship, focused prioritization of changes, strong technical/domain skills and a robust change management process are essential for implementation of large programs and evolution of IT. Broadly, the change initiatives can be categorized under the following heads:

- Programs to leverage advanced technology and innovation
- Integration programs related to mergers and acquisition
- Programs related to regulatory, risk and compliance
- Programs to maintain technology currency
- Programs to enrich information and analytics

PROGRAMS TO LEVERAGE ADVANCED TECHNOLOGY AND INNOVATION

Banks may leverage advances in technology to offer product innovations, operational efficiencies or good customer experience. Use of advanced technology offers a significant competitive advantage in terms of opportunities to cut operational costs, improve customer satisfaction and retention. Some examples of technology driven programs are described below.

Advances in Customer Channels

Banks have been able to improve operational efficiencies and customer satisfaction by implementing advanced technologies in customer channels, as given below:

* Latest ATM machines offer the possibility of handling almost complete branch transactions including transfer of funds, payment of bills and standing instructions.
* The ability to interact with a teller through video facility in an ATM helps to provide a personal touch as well as additional services. This will also help banks to consolidate the teller operations to improve availability as well as reduce costs.
* Use of in-branch video facility for niche products helps to consolidate the product specialists in a centralized location and provide wider coverage.
* Mobile based access to bank accounts and payments for easy and convenient banking is on the rise. This will not only help customers move to more self-service transactions but also reduce expensive cash transactions for banks.

Service Architecture and Business Process Management

As discussed earlier, service architecture helps banks to modernize their systems landscape, and at the same time leverage their current investments in legacy technology. In this approach, legacy applications like core banking, cards and lending will be made to expose key business processes as services to other applications. Indirect channels, workflow and productivity applications can be built or enhanced using these services.

Typically IT systems are aligned based on the functionality or business domain (core banking, cards, collections etc.). However a business process, like applying for a new card, may have to cut across different functionalities available in different IT systems to complete it. Assuming that these functionalities of different IT systems are available as services, business process management will enable process definition, process execution and process monitoring by defining the orchestration between these services.

Some examples of such programs are:

- Redesigning the call centre application for an intuitive interface and better productivity by leveraging services exposed by product systems.

- Redesigning the operations application by leveraging imaging technology for scanning and electronically linking the documents to customer accounts.

- Business process driven origination process where a process can be configured, executed and monitored using a BPM tool.

INTEGRATION PROGRAMS RELATED TO MERGERS AND ACQUISITION

Bank mergers and acquisitions are common in every country. At the end of a merger or acquisition, the target bank is left to deal with the IT systems landscapes of both banks. Depending on the bank strategy they may go in for full integration, partial integration or minimalistic integration. The level of integration depends on a number of factors like branding and product strategy of the merged entity.

- **Branding strategy:** The combined bank may choose to merge the brands into one of the existing entities. To some extent, such a business decision will allow better and faster integration of the systems.

- **Product strategy:** Even though the broad range of offerings is the same, the exact product features and attributes may be different in the merging entities. The combined entity may decide to merge the products offered by mapping the products of one entity to the closest matching product in the combined entity. This approach will help banks to retain one of the IT systems (with minimal changes) and migrate data into it from the merging entity. However in certain cases, banks may have to retain the products of both the entities 'as-is', either to reduce customer attrition or due to regulatory restrictions to keep the service levels.

Let us look at the level of integration options for the merged entity.

- **Complete integration:** In the target state both the merging banks' systems will consolidate onto a common platform. The chosen platform for the target state is enhanced to cater to the product requirements of the combined entity. It is also possible to choose the target state for each application. For example, it may be decided to use core banking from one entity and card applications from another entity based on various considerations like technology currency, maintainability and scalability. If the bank has decided to retain both the brands then the target platform will need to have multi brand capability to support such requirements.

- **Partial integration:** Banks may choose to integrate partly so as to keep the integration costs minimum as part of the merger. In this case, applications like channels, product systems will be selectively integrated based on the ease of integration and return on-investment. In such cases, complete integration is deferred to a later date.

- **Minimalistic integration:** Mergers and acquisitions with an intention for potential sale after turnaround will not warrant either partial or complete integration. In such a scenario both the systems will be continued to run 'as-is'. However some integration of enterprise applications like finance and HR need to be carried out to manage financial statements and human resources.

Another important factor in such programs is data migration. Before the combined entity can go live on the integrated application, data from the retiring application need to be migrated into the target state application. This is a very complex and intensive process and the following points have to be taken into consideration:

- There may be issues like quality, completeness and correctness in the retiring application data which cannot be handled by the target application. Hence it is required to validate, cleanse and enrich the data from the retiring application before they can be loaded to the combined application.

- There can be differences in the data models of the two merging systems that need to be addressed before migration can start. Data from the retiring application need to be transformed into the target data model before they can be loaded to the target application.
- Data have to be loaded into the target application without compromising on the referential integrity including system generated keys, like customer id etc.
- Another key element to be considered in the data migration is the time taken to complete the data migration. Applications will have a large number of records to be migrated but limited permissible downtime to complete the data migration. So the time taken for migration should be estimated, and if required an incremental approach adopted. In the incremental approach historical data will be prepared well in advance (a week or month before) and only the incremental data will be migrated on the go live date.
- Several rehearsals will need to be carried out for the entire migration life cycle to validate data migration correctness. Time taken to complete the migration needs to be tracked against the available time window for production migration and necessary performance tuning measures need to be taken up, if required.

Apart from the application, consolidation banks can also realize significant savings by looking at consolidation of data centres, server consolidation and consolidation of software licenses including COTS products.

PROGRAMS RELATED TO REGULATORY, RISK AND COMPLIANCE

Regulatory, risk and compliance is a constant and key source of IT changes for banks. Regulations are continuously changing, new regulations are coming in place and hence IT systems need to be enhanced in time to be able to meet those guidelines. Some of the programs that take place here are:

- Customer master and product systems, which are the true source of customer and transaction information. This information is sent to several downstream systems like finance, risk, data warehouse etc. In these systems, data are further sliced and diced for application specific processing. However, consistency and correctness of data across the downstream systems is a major challenge especially if these systems and their data models were evolved over a period of time. Improvement in data quality and consolidation can help improve the quality of risk management and reporting for banks. Such programs involve developing the data model, improving the data quality rules and data migration.

- Improved/Additional reporting to regulators based on revised guidelines. This typically involves sourcing the data from product systems, validating, cleansing the data and preparing reports.

- Banks may also have to adapt their services and technology to comply with regulations like payment regulations, regulations on fees and charges, regulations on card security etc.

PROGRAMS TO MAINTAIN TECHNOLOGY CURRENCY

An IT system landscape will have a number of software applications, including system software like operating systems, data base systems, schedulers, configuration management systems, etc., as well as business application software like product systems, CRM, finance etc. These software products also evolve to introduce new features, leverage technological advances and improve performance. Support to earlier versions of software will be withdrawn after a certain duration post introduction of the newer version. Banks cannot afford to have out-of-support software as part of their technology landscape, so they need to implement IT projects to see that their technology currency is up-to-date, and leverage new features offered by products. Some examples are:

- Upgrade of database/operating system version.
- Upgrade of ERP applications to the current version. The software provider supplies the upgrade path and tools to assist in migration.

- Upgrade of core banking or card platform to the current version.

PROGRAMS TO ENRICH INFORMATION AND ANALYTICS

Information is a key asset for any bank. Banks can significantly leverage information assets to fine tune the strategy, track and monitor performance, identify opportunities, improve the effectiveness of sales, and manage and control the risk. A bank's capability to generate macro views across customers, products, timelines and other dimensions will help unearth the opportunities. A bank's internal information can be analyzed in relation to the information from external sources like rating agencies, information providers and social media to derive deep insights. Big data is a new technology theme that enables processing of large volumes of structured or unstructured data using distributed clusters, and enables intuitive queries on the data. Big data technology provides capabilities for unstructured data and faster response times over large volumes of data and distributed processing. Some examples of information related program are:

- Single customer view across products to be able to arrive at customer classification, cross-sell opportunities and improved customer experience in all interactions.
- Improved data warehouse/BI capabilities to address the needs of departments like marketing, risk, HR, operations etc.
- Leveraging big data technologies for information storage, query and analytics.

CHAPTER 12
Off-The-Shelf Product Options

Commercially available products enable faster time-to-market and significantly reduce the risk of bespoke implementation in terms of functionality and performance. There are a number of market products commercially available covering a large part of the banking landscape. Table 12.1 gives the sample list of products available in the market for the applications mentioned in banking architecture. This list is presented here for understanding and academic purposes only and does not contain any relative evaluation of these products. Also, this is a representative list presented here only for reference and all trademarks are the property of their respective companies.

Table 12.1 Off-the-shelf Product Options

Functional Area	Application	Product	Vendor
Indirect channels	Branch	BankFusion Teller	Misys
		TouchPoint Teller	FIS
		Ambit Branch Teller	SunGard
	Call centre	Unified Contact Center Enterprise	CISCO
		Banking Contact Center	Oracle
		Contact Center	Microsoft
Customer channels	ATM/POS	IST/Switch, Connex	FIS
		Base24	ACI
		EFT/ATM Switching	x/LINK
	Internet banking	Corillian Online	Fiserv
		Finacle e-banking	Infosys
		Online Banking	SAP
	Mobile banking	Mobile Solutions	SAP
		Finacle Mobile Banking	Infosys
		Mobile Banking	Fiserv

	Websites	Web Content Management	OpenText
		Drupal	Drupal
		WordPress	WordPress
Product systems	Customer master	Oracle Customer Hub	Oracle
		InfoSphere Master Data Management	IBM
		Master Data Management(MDM)	TIBCO
	Accounts/ Deposits	BaNCS	TCS
		Systematics	FIS
		Core Banking	SAP
	Payments	ePayment	FIS
		Global PAYplus	Fundtech
		Mass Payments	Dovetail
	Mortgages	Mortgage Lending	FIS
		BaNCS	TCS
		Finacle	Infosys
	Credit cards	Card Management System	FIS
		Electra iTX series	ElectraCard
		VisionPLUS	FirstData
Enterprise applications	Finance	E-Business Suite	Oracle
		FICO	SAP
		Financial Management	Ramco
	HR	E-Business Suite	Oracle
		HR	SAP
		HR Solutions	ADP
	CRM	Siebel	Oracle
		Dynamics CRM	Microsoft
		Salesforce	Salesforce
	Data warehouse	Data Warehouse Appliance	Teradata

		Exadata	Oracle
		IFW Data Model for banks	IBM
	Business intelligence	Cognos	IBM
		Business Objects	SAP
		OBIEE	Oracle
		HANA	SAP
		Analytics	SAS
Integration	File based	Synchrony	Axway
	Message based	WebSphere MQ	IBM
	ETL	Informatica	Informatica
		InfoSphere DataStage	IBM
	Service integration	Integration Bus	IBM
	Process integration	Business Process Management (BPM)	Pega
		Business Process Manager	IBM

Glossary

ATM - Automatic Teller Machine

BPM - Business Process Management

CRM - Customer Relationship Management

CTI - Computer Telephony Integration

DW/BI - Data Warehouse/Business Intelligence

EAI - Enterprise Application Integration

ESB - Enterprise Service Bus

IT - Information Technology

MDM - Master Data Management

SOA - Service Oriented Architecture

CPSIA information can be obtained at www.ICGtesting.com
Printed in the USA
BVOW11s2050291115

428813BV00018B/296/P